AF255721

"Mysticism is sometimes conceived of as being esoteric and removed from everyday experience. In this beautiful and moving theological reflection on two twentieth-century communities of martyrs, Maria Clara Bingemer reveals the vital mysticism of solidarity and accompaniment that was at the heart of their lives and their witness; one that continues to speak to us in our own time. An important and necessary work."

—**Douglas E. Christie**, professor of theological studies,
Loyola Marymount University

"In this beautifully translated work, Maria Clara Bingemer has joined her expertise in Ignatian discernment with a vivid recounting of how the monks of Tibhirine and the Salvadoran martyrs gave themselves over to God. This hope-filled and deeply reflective narrative allows Catholics to awaken from the mere dream of synodality to see it before their very eyes as a concrete reality in history. Three cheers for Bingemer's latest spiritual masterpiece!"

—**Peter Casarella**, professor of theology, Duke Divinity School

"This book is a timely reflection on the relationship of contemplation and action. Maria Clara Bingemer gives us a window into a new style of mysticism that is open to the divine in the other and simultaneously immersed in a violent world. The witness of these two communities inspires a profound hope that living for others is possible."

—**William T. Cavanaugh**, professor of Catholic studies, DePaul University

"Taking readers into a space of quiet and stillness, this book invites us to journey into the worlds of Christian De Chergé and Ignacio Ellacuría, to know more intimately these two extraordinary disciples. Their prayer, thought, and leadership crossed boundaries of difference by which they offered and continue to offer the world an exquisite gift. Maria Clara Bingemer richly honors their gift in these pages. A wonderous, spiritual feast."

—**Nancy Pineda-Madrid**, chair of Catholic theology, Loyola Marymount University

Mysticism and Witness in Koinonia

Mysticism and Witness in Koinonia

Inspiration from the Martyrdom of Two Twentieth-Century Communities

Maria Clara Bingemer

TRANSLATED BY
Suzana Regina Moreira

CASCADE *Books* · Eugene, Oregon

MYSTICISM AND WITNESS IN KOINONIA
Inspiration from the Martyrdom of Two Twentieth-Century Communities

Cascade Books
An Imprint of Wipf and Stock Publishers
199 W. 8th Ave., Suite 3
Eugene, OR 97401

www.wipfandstock.com

PAPERBACK ISBN: 978-1-6667-5264-9
HARDCOVER ISBN: 978-1-6667-5265-6
EBOOK ISBN: 978-1-6667-5266-3

Cataloguing-in-Publication data:

Names: Bingemer, Maria Clara Luchetti, author. | Moreira, Suzana Regina, translator.

Title: Mysticism and witness in koinonia : inspiration from the martyrdom of two twentieth-century communities / by Maria Clara Bingemer ; translated by Suzana Regina Moreira.

Description: Eugene, OR : Cascade Books, 2023 | Includes bibliographical references and index.

Identifiers: ISBN 978-1-6667-5264-9 (paperback) | ISBN 978-1-6667-5265-6 (hardcover) | ISBN 978-1-6667-5266-3 (ebook)

Subjects: LCSH: Witness bearing (Christianity). | Martyrdom—Christianity—History—20th century. | Trappists—Algeria—Tibehirine—Biography. | Notre Dame de l'Atlas (Monastery : Tibehirine, Algeria). | Christian martyrs—Algeria—Tibehirine—Biography. | Jesuits—Political activity—El Salvador—History—20th century. | Universidad Centroamericana José Simeón Cañas—History—20th century. | Victims of state-sponsored terrorism—El Salvador—Biography. | Martyrs—El Salvador—Biography.

Classification: BV4520 .B49 2023 (print) | BV4520 .B49 (ebook)

11/07/23

Contents

Introduction | 1

Chapter I: The Religious Community: Co-Living and Witnessing | 7

From the Hermit Life to the Cenobitic Life   8

Contemplative Life and Active Life   10

The Trappist and Its Monastic Experience   13

The Society of Jesus: A Religious Experience for Modern Times   14

Ex-centric Communities?   16

Chapter II: The Trappist Community of Tibhirine | 22

Continuous Praise and Community Prayer   24

Ora et Labora in an Islamic Country   30

A Contemplative Community in Dialogue
with Another Religion   33

The True Spirit of the Community of Tibhirine:
Service, Peace, and Discernment   37

Christian De Chergé: Prior, Mystic, and Martyr   40

Mysticism and Thinking of Christian De Chergé   47

A Community in the State of "Epiclesis"   62

A Testament to the Twenty-First Century   67

The Free Choice of a Prayer Community   70

CONTENTS

Chapter III: The UCA as an Intellectual, Apostolic, and
 Community Project | 73

What Is a Confessional University?   78

The Inspiration of the Historical-Ecclesial Moment
of the Continent   80

The Role of the Jesuits in the Post-Conciliar
Latin American Movement   86

The Educational Apostolate of the Society of Jesus
in the Post-Conciliar Church   89

UCA: A University at the Service of Social Transformation   94

Ignacio Ellacuría: Philosopher, Theologian, and Dean of UCA   100

The Salvation of and in History   103

An Intellectual Life at the Service of the Poor   105

Ignacio Ellacuría: A "Mystical Thought"   110

Living and Dying in Community   118

The Meaning and Legacy of the Martyrdom
of the UCA Community   120

Prayer to Ignacio Ellacuría   124

Conclusion: Martyrdom as a Community Liturgy | 127

Bibliography | 137
Index of Names | 151

Introduction

Theology is born from inspiration. It often takes shape from an intuition. I believe it was an intuition that led me one day to approach these two communities and to fall in love with them, their history, their mysticism, and their witness.

I was close to the Universidad Católica de El Salvador (UCA) community for some time. The connection with the Jesuits made me observe closely all the work of Ignacio Ellacuría and his companions. As a theology student in the 80s, the books of Jon Sobrino were a strong and succulent theological meal that made us think, pray, and vibrate. Later, I met Jon himself, in meetings for the collection *Teologia e Libertação* (*Theology and Liberation*), which took place in Petrópolis, Correias, São Paulo.

We would talk about life, work, and music, and we sang along with others to the sounds of an acoustic guitar. Theology is also made that way. Jon Sobrino, the Basque-Salvadoran theologian, was setting the stage for Latin-American theology alongside Gustavo Gutiérrez, Leonardo Boff, and many others. The categories he was creating from his work in El Salvador would later become central: the victims, theology as *intellectus amoris*, the imperative of the poor descending from the cross, and many other categories that still today guide the theological path in our continent. But he also had a beautiful voice to sing spiritual Spanish and Latin-American songs. He told me privately that as a novice he already had solos in the choir, and that music always inspired him.

I also met Ignacio Ellacuría. I only saw him once in Madrid, where I was accompanying my colleague Lina Boff, who would be participating with him in a television show. He went to the hotel where we were to visit Lina. We talked briefly and he dedicated a book for me, which I have kept to this day. Charismatic, with a penetrating gaze and tenacious humor, his clear and sharp intelligence shone through his demeanor and in his words.

In November 1989, upon entering my house after returning from university, my mother told me that Leonardo Boff had called several times and he seemed languished on the phone. I called him immediately and received the news of the massacre of the whole Jesuit community. Leonardo said with a heavy voice: "They killed all of them. They are martyrs." I still remember how that struck my heart.

After that, I reencountered Jon Sobrino in meetings with theologians, at conferences of the Brazilian Society of Theology, and other occasions. I was always impressed by the faithfulness with which he dedicated all his efforts to theological thought in memory of those martyrs. It was a true obsession to make sure that their witness of faith and all it meant did not fade in the minds of the people of God.

In 2007, I became part of the editorial board of the *Concilium* journal and there I met my friend Jon more often and with more depth. Our talks were longer. I had the honor to work with him in the organization of some journal editions. We would sing at night, along with other work companions, including Andrés Queiruga, Silvia Scatena, Susan Ross, and Lisa Cahill. Jon was still full of musical gifts and lavished it to all.

His diabetes weighed on him more than before, and age made him more sensitive. He felt tired but still worked a lot, though in a slower rhythm than before. In 2010, he invited me to participate in a conference at the theological seminary for the 30th anniversary of the martyrdom of Archbishop Oscar Romero. It was a deep experience I will never forget, visiting the graves of the Jesuits and of Elba and Celina in the garden of roses at the university, as well as visiting the Romero Center, the crypt where his remains are found. It was amazing to see people from all over the world, young and old, touched by the subversive memory of the martyr archbishop who spoke prophetically and who was assassinated at the moment of consecration, during the Eucharist. Those holy places would never leave my memory.

Later, I was in Chicago on a sabbatical. There I planned, along with Peter Casarella, to organize an event about mysticism and witness. It took place in 2012, hosted with the partnership of the Pontifical Catholic University of Rio de Janeiro and De Paul University. Jon was invited to speak on the theme that he was dedicating his life to. The auditorium was packed.

More than 300 people heard him witnessing with respect and emotion and then gave him a standing ovation.

In 2015, the Second Vatican Council and the *Concilium* journal celebrated their 50th anniversary. I was in charge of organizing the symposium, followed by a meeting of the editorial board at the Pontifical Catholic University of Rio de Janeiro. Jon came and gave one of the conferences. He was tired and all the medicine he had to take jeopardized his energy. He spoke with a weak voice, but transmitted the full message that accompanied him since the day in Thailand when he received the news over the phone from his friend Julian Filochowski that his whole community had been murdered.

On that day, in the auditorium of the Pontifical Catholic University of Rio de Janeiro, he told more than 400 people gathered at the venue: there are pasts that are destined for museums or that bury life, and there are pasts that unfold life. That is how he perceived the role of theology, which should be inspired from these fertile pasts to become—according to his own expression—not so much about texts, but about witnesses.

I have not seen him since. I follow him with affection over the news I receive and I always have him present in my thoughts. With him, unbounding from his own person, is the whole UCA community, his community, and just as well the mysticism and the martyrdom that those men—and their brothers—lived in a university situated in the small country of El Salvador.

My encounter with the Trappists of Tibhirine happened much later. In 2009, my husband and I were in Aix en Provence, France, to visit our youngest daughter who lived there. One of her friends recommended us a movie that, according to him, we absolutely had to watch. The title was *Des hommes et des dieux*, by the French director Xavier Beauvois. The fact that this young man, who did not have faith nor proximity with any church, was deeply touched and moved by the movie of Xavier Beauvois called my attention. The movie was about a Trappist community in Algeria that was murdered in the '90s and whose kidnapping and death impacted all of France.

Later I recalled that I had seen news about it, which I had only lightly skimmed through. The movie experience was extremely profound and unforgettable. The beauty of the story and the cinematography, made by an atheist director and with only two actors who were believers while the rest also had no faith, surprised me for being so convincing. The movie made me throb, ache, and cry. The next day, I started to ceaselessly search for bibliography, information, readings, commentaries, anything related to that community of the Atlas Mountains.

I long dedicated myself to the witness of Brother Lucas, the doctor who took care of more than 100 patients per day. I read, cherishing the beautiful and poetic writings of father Christophe Lebreton, who was only 45 years old at the time of the kidnapping and murder. But foremost, I dove in with all the attention and passion I was capable of on the writings of Prior Christian de Chergé. His imminent figure as a mystic, philosopher, theologian, and thinker fascinated me right from the beginning. His love for Islam, his continuous and passionate efforts to dialogue with this other tradition that he lived by free choice, all impressed me increasingly more as I read his writings.

I had the opportunity to reflect and discuss those details of the monks' relationship with Islam with other mysticism scholars, especially with a group that gathered annually for the memorable meetings of the *Seminário da Floresta* (Seminary of the Forest) at the city of Juiz de Fora, as well as with members of the research group *Apophatike* of interdisciplinary studies about mysticism that I am part of. I wrote and published work about his thought and mysticism.

The intuition of writing this book by approaching the two seemingly different communities, with such diverse charisms—one being apostolic, situated in a university, the other being contemplative, in a monastery on top of a mountain—came to me after my research in Chicago, which resulted in the publication of the book *O mistério e o mundo* by Editora Rocco, in 2013, which was discussed in various forums and groups.

I felt that the intuition I developed there, about which I researched and reflected on, was gaining shape and giving more fruit. Among the central points of my research was the realization that contemporary mystics are not situated only nor mainly in the cloisters and clearly religious or ecclesial spaces. On the contrary, they can be found amidst very secular environments, compromised and committed to challenges that come from society and the culture of their time. It was then that the two martyr communities appeared to me clearly as concrete cases of this mysticism.

The Jesuits of UCA ran the university with academic excellence and high-end research. But at the same time they were focused on the unfair and oppressed reality of the country where this university was located: El Salvador, the center of a continent divided by poverty and inequality. The Jesuits denounced this state of affairs and positioned themselves against those responsible for it. They turned the university toward the reality of their country in order to help transform it. They followed the path of Monsignor Oscar Romero, and just as they followed him in life and testimony, they followed him equally in the martyrial destiny.

The Trappists of Tibhirine were a contemplative community, with times for prayer distributed throughout the day, while working on the land and selling the product of their work at the local market. In addition, they developed close friendships with the local community that they had great affection for. But their conception of monastic life and of what a monastery should be was open and inclusive. It implied the unrestricted participation and hospitality with Muslims who would find space for their prayers, hold meetings, and share faith, word, and prayer. They united social commitment with integration and intercultural and religious dialogue. The medical clinic of Brother Lucas who attended, without ceasing, the poor patients who came to him, was part of the Lien de Paix group, which the prior coordinated alongside other Catholic and Muslim religious people.

What moved the communities that we discuss here, what constituted their mysticism and was also the cause of their martyrdom, was a profound commitment to the difference of the other, with their vulnerability, their needs, and the calling that implied. Thus, in their immense differences, these communities are close together, connected, corresponding to one another. Through different charisms, different nationalities, and diverse situations, both converge in the desire to encounter the other to enter into communion with him or her.

The conclusion of my book *O mistério e o mundo* was in that direction. The mysticism of today finds its seal of authenticity in the unbiddable desire to enter into communion with the pain of the other. At this point, both communities fraternize for having lived this desire until the radicalism of martyrdom.

The reader must forgive me for such an autobiographical introduction. But this is another conclusion of my research on mysticism and theology, or on mystical theology. You cannot separate the theologian from his or her biography. The biography, the history of faith, the spirituality that animates those who experience God in a profound and loving way, are inseparable from their thinking and their action. Mysticism and knowledge, mysticism and ethics, are inseparable.

We hope that the testimony of these two admirable communities may help in understanding this truth that makes itself so palpable in the world in which we live and that can be a driving force to renew the church in its desire for conversion and service to society.

Maria Clara Lucchetti Bingemer
September 13, 2017
Feast of Saint John Chrysostom

CHAPTER I

The Religious Community

Co-Living and Witnessing

RELIGIOUS LIFE WITHIN THE Catholic Church has some characteristics that distinguish it from other collectives within the ecclesial body. Inspired by the Holy Spirit, some of the faithful Christians are called to radically follow Jesus Christ through the profession of evangelical counsels, by vows or other sacred bonds, in a stable way of life approved by the church.[1] They possess a special charism in the ecclesial community and contribute to its life and mission according to the nature, spirit, and purpose of their respective institutes. For this reason there is a wide range of institutes of consecrated life in the church, which commit to a life rule according to a certain aspect of the life of Jesus Christ, manifesting it to the world with special emphasis. Thus, for example, there are religious orders and congregations that identify with the life of Jesus Christ in one of its aspects, manifesting him by praying on the mountain, or by proclaiming the kingdom of God, or doing good for people, or yet living among men and women in the world, always doing the will of the Father.[2] Likewise, the institutes may be run by clerics or lay Christians according to the founder's project and recognition by the authority of the church.[3]

A religious person is therefore:

> A faithful Christian who follows the evangelical counsels of poverty, chastity, and obedience, by profession of vows, living a life in common with an institute of consecrated life, a life-form approved by the church. Before the Second Vatican Council, many religious

1. *Code of Canon Law*, c. 573.

2. *Code of Canon Law*, c. 577.

3. McDermott, "Consecrated Life," 155.

people lived very similar lives, with similar schedules, customs, spirituality, prayer, and so on. With the Second Vatican Council, there was an orientation given to the institutes to rediscover their roots and return to the charism of their founder or foundress.[4]

It is worthwhile, however, to go back to the origins, the beginnings of this desire and charism that has conquered the heart and life of so many Christians who live their baptism in such a way that they would come to adopt a different way of life, namely to gather in community and be joined by the vows to the paradigm that is Jesus Christ.

From the Hermit Life to the Cenobitic Life

The monastic movement was quite important in the Christian church. It all began after the Constantine reform during the fourth century and the cessation of persecutions that resulted in thousands of martyrs. The first monks and nuns were hermits,[5] but very quickly several ascetic Christians began to gather in monastic communities. They passed from the hermit life to the cenobitic life.

Cenobites are religious people who, in contrast to the hermits or anchorites, live their lives in common. The precise use of the word "cenobite" (from the Greek κοινός, common, and βίος, life), however, is limited to members of monastic communities whose lives are mainly in the cenobitic monastery and not in the apostolic work.[6]

Since the Middle Ages in the eleventh century, these communities have been based on the rule of St. Benedict,[7] but in the thirteenth century a

4. Shea, "Religious (Men and Women)," 88.

5. Hermits are people who have withdrawn in solitude to lead a religious life consecrated to God and prayer. The term is derived through ancient French and Latin, from Greek ἐρεμίτης. Although there were probably lonely "avant la lettre" Christians, an Egyptian named Paul was the first to popularize hermitic life. Since the beginning of the fourth century, this life has been one of the standardized forms, especially in the East, in which Christian asceticism has manifested itself. Donahue, "Hermits," 799–800.

6. Donahue, "Cenobites," 334.

7. St. Benedict of Nurcia, born Benedict of Norcia (in Italian: Benedetto de Norcia; in Latin: Benedictus; Norcia, Ostrogothic Kingdom, c. 480–Abbey of Monte Cassino, c. 547) was a monk, founder of the Order of Benedictines, one of the largest monastic orders in the world. He was the creator of the Rule of St. Benedict, one of the most important and widely used monastic life regulations, the inspiration of many other religious communities. He was the twin brother of St. Scholastic. He was appointed patron of Europe by Pope Paul VI in 1964, and also patron of Germany. He was revered not only

new model for monasticism emerged in Western Europe. The growth of the population and the struggle to survive left a growing number of people in poverty. In northern Italy, Francis of Assisi felt the call to serve these people. Francis initiated what is known as *mendicant monasticism.* The Franciscans were known as a mendicant order that lived by alms and begging for daily sustenance, both for themselves and for the poor who lived with them. The mendicants did not wish to possess properties and so did not live in a monastery as such. Instead, they dwelled in the world, and were known as friars instead of monks. They worked hard to try to alleviate the suffering faced by the poorest inhabitants of Europe at the time.[8]

Monastic orders continued to develop throughout Europe. Currently, there are more than seventy-five different orders in the Catholic Church. These include groups such as Cistercian, Capuchin, Augustinian, and Trappist, along with various groups of women, such as the Carmelites, Poor Clares, and Benedictines. Subsequently, orders that had begun with another configuration and charism became contemplative, such as the Sisters of Mercy, who began as an order of nurses.

Monasticism has played a key role throughout the history of Christianity. More importantly, monks and nuns have been responsible for the education and preservation of ancient texts, have acted in the area of health, in nursing and in hospitals, orphanages, and other social ministries around the world. And consecrated life—either contemplative or active—nowadays is always ahead in the ecclesial journey, taking avant-garde positions in the main struggles of the church's testimony and mission.[9]

---

by Catholics, but also by Orthodox and Anglicans. He was the founder of the Monte Cassino Abbey in Italy, destroyed during World War II and later restored. Benedict is commemorated on the Catholic calendar on July 11, when his relics were moved to the Abbey of Saint-Benoît-sur-Loire. See "Benedict of Nursia."

8. Another begging group was born in the thirteenth century as well. The Dominicans were founded by a Spaniard named Domingos de Guzmán in 1220 The Dominicans are known as the Order of Preachers, as Domingos traveled the countryside preaching and begging. He was also involved in the suppression of those considered heretics of the church, especially in southern France. Because of this emphasis on preaching and teaching, Domingos and his followers, the Dominicans, eventually became the predominant source of teachers for Europe's first universities.

9. Suffice it to cite the countless testimonies of religious men or women who gave their lives to the end, whether by turning back into very poor communities or by violent death due to their evangelical commitment.

Contemplative Life and Active Life

Contemplative life is a term used to indicate a life characterized by solitude and prayer. However, careful distinction must be made between a life of solitude with very real, spontaneous prayer—that any Christian can decide to undertake—and a state of life officially called "contemplative," in which everything is officially organized in order to create an atmosphere of prayer and stillness. This implies a cloistered life, in a space away from other spaces in the world and society, in which, through the exercise of prayer, mortification, and work, somehow connected with the cloister and everything turned to interior contemplation, God can penetrate easily and effectively all of life. By decreasing or even extinguishing external stimulations, the internal stimulation for the encounter with God grows exponentially.

If we look at the etymology of terms, we see that the *theoreticus*, a Greek adjective, which came to be translated as *contemplativus* or *speculativus* in Latin, derives from the Greek *theoria*, which is understood as a contemplation. An idea of vision, or to see, is suggested in both languages, and most scholars agree that the Greek word is a compound of two roots, *Thea* and *oram*, which do not imply vision only, but also observation and investigation.[10] Mary Elizabeth Mason adds that the idea of connecting these with the word *Theos* (God) was proposed by the Peripatetics, but she understands—following A. J. Festugière—that *Theoros* (the one who sees) and its compounds soon acquired religious connotations.[11] Following this thought, a *theoros*, in the sense of someone who approaches to observe a religious rite, came to be regarded as a free approach of divinity itself that generates joy for the union with a god.[12]

Mason also draws attention to the fact that the equivalent for *activus* is *praktikos*, which means "apt to do, concerned with action, practical." She recalls that in the writings of Aristotle there is the occasional use of this term in contrast to *theoreticos*.[13] Plato was familiar with both terms. But it would be a mistake, according to Mason, to sustain that both ideas are opposed to one another. That is because knowledge, learning, and all sorts of acquired skills were, in general, due to action. It is sufficient to remember

---

10. Festugière, *Contemplation et vie contemplative*, 13; Mason, *Active Life*, 11.

11. Mason, *Active Life*, 11.

12. Festugière, *Contemplation et vie contemplative*, 13; and Mason, *Active Life*, 12. Festugière adds that in the original theory he designates a model of sociability; and later a kind of seclusion (*Contemplation et vie contemplative*, 17).

13. *Nicomachean Ethics*, cited in Mason, *Active Life*, 12.

the writings of the classical Greeks, such as Homer, Pindar, and Euripides, where we can see the courageous heroes in action, not just theorists. The radical separation of one and the other is not coherent with the phenomenon of consecrated life as a whole in Christianity.

In the third century, Origen identified the active life with Martha of Bethany and the contemplative life with her sister Mary, according to what long has been the interpretation of Luke 10:38–42. In fact, in the parable, what Jesus criticizes in Martha is not her service of arranging the house to receive him, but rather the agitation and annoyance with which she does it, to the point of questioning her own sister about why she doesn't help her.[14] The two attitudes, in reality—to serve and to hear and contemplate—are legitimized by the Master and the Christian community. So much so that in chapter 11 of the Gospel of John, before the death of Lazarus, Jesus dialogues with Martha and her lips are the ones to confess the faith in the messianism of Jesus as the son of God, a confession similar to that of Peter in Matt 16:16.[15]

What should be observed, more than "the best" part chosen by Mary is the word "part." Mary and her choice do not form a totality, but rather a part, just like Martha. If we unite them, the result is not two lives, but one life, a totality that is the Christian life, the life in Christ.[16] This is the life that Christ came to bring: his own life, the life that is recognized and embraced by both the contemplatives, who make life itself of their contemplation and knowledge, and of the actives, as Paul in his apostolic ministry says without blinking: "For to me life is Christ."[17] Or Ignatius of Loyola, who in the Meditation of the Two Standards in the *Spiritual Exercises*, urges the exercisers to make the following petition: "Ask for what I want; And here I must ask for knowledge of the deceit of the bad commander, and help to keep me away; and knowledge of the *true life* that shows the upmost and true captain, and grace to imitate him."[18]

St. Paul used the Greek word "askein"[19] to express the practical question of "working" for salvation, of the pursuit of perfection, or to make a

---

14. Mason, *Active Life*, 83. Cf. Dupont, *Marthe et Marie.*

15. Cf. the comment on this perícope by Tepedino, *As discípulas de Jesus.*

16. Mason, *Active Life*, 110–11.

17. Phil 1:21.

18. St. Ignatius of Loyola, *Spiritual Exercises*, n. 139. The italics are ours.

19. Asceticism: many unbelievers will say that only an ascetic could get rid of temptation. This word comes from the Greek *asketes*, "one who exercises, athlete," and from

spiritual effort to purify one's conscience in order to approach God. Origen was in turn the first to apply the word "ascetic" to Christians who practiced virginity and dedicated themselves to works of mortification. With St. Augustine, the active life as a term became almost synonymous with ascetic, understood as an effort, making it consistent in the practice of virtues, as beyond contemplation of the truth.[20]

Active life reaches a new level when it begins to worry about the caring of souls. Since Augustine's time, authors have pointed out that bishops, to whom the care of souls belong legitimately and officially, lead the active life in its broadest sense, as well as the contemplative life, since all their activity must be richly impregnated by contemplation. It follows that the more those who are not bishops exercise their active lives more fully, the more they will participate in the care of souls, a work proper to bishops. This is why St. Thomas can classify these religious orders, whose concern is to give others the fruit of their contemplation in the first place. Historically, at the beginning, religious orders were concerned only with the perfection of their own members. Gradually, the needs of souls—the later so-called "healing of souls"—forced them to carry out the apostolate proper to the bishops. Religious orders, such as Franciscans and Dominicans in the thirteenth century, were founded to do the work that bishops could no longer do alone. The revolutionary Society of Jesus (1540), which set a new standard for many of the most modern religious institutes, moved into any area where it was necessary for the good of souls, whether bodily and spiritual works of mercy, or preaching and the administration of the Sacraments.[21]

Obviously, the term "active life" is an analogous term. In a non-spiritual sense it would be the opposite of collected, silent. In a spiritual sense it is ambiguous, because it can mean the opposite of contemplative life or life that springs from contemplation. When used in the context of spirituality as a unique term, generally it refers to the life of virtue, the pursuit of virtue, the life dedicated to the bodily and spiritual works of mercy, and all those things that are indirectly related to charity.

In fact, the highest state of Christian life is one that consists in the union of the two lives (considered more as states of the soul or as states or orientations of the soul resulting in the respective attitudes of the mind and

---

askein, "to do, to exercise." To be an ascetic means to be austere. It is one who does self-denial as a form of discipline.

20. Mason, *Active Life,* 110–11.

21. Mason, *Active Life,* 110–11.

consequently in its characteristic exterior practice). This union is one in which the charity of contemplative life flows into the active life in order to motivate, inspire, control, and direct its practice.[22]

The higher criterion for evaluating the contemplative life and the active life is actually the increase of charity, of love. Since the essence of Christian perfection consists in the increase of charity, which grows proportionally with the sanctifying grace, this same charity is the most important and decisive factor. Both the activity and contemplation, or any combination of both, must be examined according to their value and ability to increase sanctifying grace and be able to act with more charity and love toward others.

The Trappist and Its Monastic Experience

The Cistercian Order of Strict Observance (OCSO), popularly known as the Order of the Trappists, originated in 1098, when Robert de Molesme, Alberico, and Stephen Harding took a group from the flourishing Benedictine Abbey in Molesme to the Cister forest in the Diocese of Chalon-sur-Saone (Dijon) in France. These men were determined to seek God by following the Rule of St. Benedict in its fullness and radicality. His Constitutions and Statutes are based on St. Stephen's Charta Caritatis, and on the uses and definitions of the Cister ancient general chapters. Like all other monastic orders, after the Second Vatican Council the Cistercian Order of Strict Observance, as it is now called, undertook the writing of new constitutions and statutes, and work was completed in Holyoke, Massachusetts, in 1983. The order continued to grow, and by the year 2000 it had over one hundred men's houses and nearly seventy women's houses, with most of the new foundations taking place in Africa and Latin America. The order maintains its strictly contemplative orientation, while at the same time sharing its contemplative heritage through its inns, membership programs, and the dissemination of its contemplative spirituality, as well as through its many writers, notably Thomas Merton, among others. Without a doubt, to these today must be added the name of the prior of the Tibhirine community, Christian de Chergé, whose writings we will study in this book.[23] Not only are there works written by him that reflect the Trappist spirit in

22. Mason, *Active Life*, 113.

23. Chergé, *Les vies des saints*; Chergé, *L'Autre que nous attendons*; Chergé, *Dieu pour tout jour*; Chergé, *L'échelle mystique du dialogue*, 1–26; Chergé, *L'Invincible espérance*.

these post-council times, but there are also numerous works—books and articles—written about him and his work.[24]

The Trappists start the day while it is still dark at 3 or 4 in the morning, and end it around 7 or 8 in the evening. Several hours each day are devoted to the Divine Office or Liturgy of the Hours and the communal mass. Four to six hours are reserved for manual labor to enable the community to support itself. The rest of the seventeen-hour day is devoted to contemplative prayer, *lectio divina*, and study. Trappists lead a strictly contemplative life on the cenobitic model. Silence is highly valued and prevails in their monasteries. The diet is very simple: it excludes meat and encourages fasting. Simplicity, the characteristic virtue of Trappists, marks everything in their life. An extreme aesthetic sense and refined taste are combined to this simplicity, which is a striking feature of their beautiful abbeys and monasteries.

The Society of Jesus: A Religious Experience for Modern Times

The Society of Jesus is a religious order of priests and brothers, popularly known as Jesuits, a name that was originally descriptive and indicated the connotation of "falsehood" and cunning in a negative sense.[25] The order grew out of the activity of its founder, Iñigo (Ignatius) de Loyola, former military officer in the service of the King of Spain, converted after a war wound and a long convalescence.[26] He later joined six companions who, on the Montmartre Hill in Paris on August 15, 1534, cast their vows of poverty, chastity, and apostolic work in the Holy Land; or, if this latter plan were not to prove viable, as it so happened, they would make a vow of readiness to any apostolic mission ordered by the pope. The purpose of the company is the salvation of souls and the life of perfection of the Jesuits as individuals, of the company as an apostolic body, and of the whole human race. The organization of the Jesuits, their way of life, and the ministries they exercise are all directed toward this goal. The official orientations of the order in these matters are contained in a body of writings known

24. The reader can consult these references in the bibliography at the end of the book.

25. According to the Dicionário Priberam da Língua Portuguesa: "a person who is faked or disguised = Hypocrite," 2008–2013.

26. Cf. countless biographies of Iñigo (alias Inácio) Lopez de Loyola. Among them especially, Idígoras, *Inácio de Loyola*; in addition to Ignatius, *Autobiography*, dictated by the saint himself.

collectively as the Institute (Institutum). They are mainly comprised of papal documents pertaining to the Society: the Constitutions of the Society of Jesus and the *Spiritual Exercises*, both composed by Saint Ignatius, in addition to the rules and statutes of the general congregations, and the instructions of the general superiors. Its members are either priests or candidates preparing for the priesthood, or supporting brothers, whose duties include a wide variety of ministries. After joining the order, they all spend two full years of spiritual formation in a novitiate, preceded, in the case of the brothers, by a six-month postulancy.[27]

In its structure, the Society of Jesus draws heavily on older orders, although it introduces several original features, some of which have been reaffirmed in more recent General Congregations. These include: high centralization of authority; vitality of the General Superior of the Order;[28] probationary period lasting several years (many more than other religious orders) and preceding the perpetual vows; graduation of members at various levels; prohibition of accepting honorary positions or privileges in the church; private recitation of the Divine Office rather than community and choral recitation; absence of regular penances or mandatory fasts for all; use of a nonproprietary religious habit, but modeled on that of the secular clergy of each region;[29] absence of a second order, or feminine branch; and absence of a third order of lay people. Due to the nature of its foundation, Ignatius particularly stressed the virtue of obedience. His expressions, characterizing the Jesuit's obedience, make use of images as radical as blind obedience, like that of a corpse, or the staff in the hand of an old man. These were not originally coined by him, but are figurative phrases taken and uttered in the inspiration of ancient monastic traditions, which must be interpreted in this light. Jesuit obedience is not military but religious, and this is very clear to Ignatius of Loyola.[30]

The Jesuits were not the first religious order to distinguish themselves as teachers and educators, but they were the first with constitutions that included educational work in general as a regular task. Ignatius' other innovation was the extension of ministries, excluding secular companies

27. Broderick and Lapomarda, "Jesuits," 779–81.

28. This characteristic was first broken in 2005 when then-general Father Peter-Hans Kolvenbach resigned. And then by his successor, Father Adolfo Nicolas, who resigned in 2016.

29. St. Ignatius' instruction is to dress like the honest priests of the place. Cf. *Constituições da Companhia e Normas Complementares*, 168.

30. Broderick and Lapomarda, "Jesuits," 782.

and businesses and political involvement. In this sense, the founder saw the mission of the society as capable of embracing all kinds of apostolic efforts in all parts of the world, provided they tended toward the greatest glory of God. The motto of the order is A.M.D.G. (*Ad Majorem Dei gloriam* = to the greatest glory of God). Ignatian spirituality, rooted in the *Spiritual Exercises*, has always been the spirituality lived by the Society, and thanks to the apostolic action of the Jesuits, it had a profound effect on the development of modern spirituality.[31]

From this we could conclude very quickly and superficially that the two communities we want to study have nothing in common: one being contemplative, with special rules of silence, times of common prayer, penance, etc.; the other being missionary to the point where Ignatius says in the Constitutions that the Jesuit who has pronounced the last and perpetual vows can be dispensed—if the demands of the mission are clearly evidenced—from daily prayer, though never from the examination of conscience, the practice through which the apostolic discernment is made, which is the content of the "account of conscience" practice of the society.[32]

If so, is their brutal and violent death the only resemblance between these two mystic and witnessing communities? Is their martyrdom just the kind of death both suffered? Or on the contrary, is their death a spiritual but very logical consequence of their life and mysticism that animated both and the vital choices they consequently made? Are not both communities linked through a very beautiful and deep process that brings them together?

Ex-centric Communities?

In what sense do the two communities we intend to study here have common features? First, indeed, they are both Christian communities, therefore church cells. Like every group of Christians that come together, they believe that Jesus Christ is in their midst.[33] It is constitutive of Christianity

31. Broderick and Lapomarda, "Jesuits," 782.

32. This examination consists of opening and fully communicating to the superior all the movements felt within him so that the superior can then send him wherever God's greatest glory is and the work best suited to what God desires for him. The examination of personal conscience, as well as the private examination, will then be the way by which the Jesuit can open before his superior his apostolic and missionary desires. Cf. *Constituições da Companhia de Jesus e Normas Complementares*, nn. 155, 1, 2.

33. "For where two or three are gathered together in my name, there am I in the midst of them" (Matt 18:20).

to live the faith in community. Far from being something individualistic and lonely, which takes people away from their peers, Christianity is gregarious, requiring and demanding community.

By the simple fact, therefore, of claiming to themselves the name of Christians, belonging to two religious orders of the Catholic Church, one of the most important and numerous denominations of historical Christianity, the Trappists and the Jesuits demonstrate that their communal ties are part of their same identity and make them have more common ground than differences.

However, both the communities we study here, the Tibhirine Trappists and the El Salvador Jesuits, live different styles of community than the other communities in their family or religious order. And this difference brings them closer than what differentiates them. Both lived a community that understood itself as extended and ex-centric.

Extended because it housed and recognized as members—at some level at least—people who did not belong to the religious order itself. In the case of the Trappists, the inhabitants of the village surrounding the monastery were not even Christians but Muslims, or even the participants of the Ribat el Salam group (Peace link). The monastic community understood itself as inextricably linked with this larger community by faith, prayer, and the desire for communion. This wish was brought out and made clearer and stronger with the arrival of Christian de Chergé and then with his election and action as prior. But it cannot be said that this was absent from the community before, because had it not been several decades since Brother Lucas served the village people as well as anyone who came forward needing medical care as a brother? Is it not a fact that the monks participated in the lives of the residents, in their family, and even religious parties? Is it not affirmed and reaffirmed by all the works that comment and describe the life in the monastery of Notre Dame de l'Atlas that several other religious groups, linked by the same dedication and the same love for the church of Algeria, formed wider circles around the monastery?

I believe it can be said, without fear of forcing the statement, that the Tibhirine community is a community with concentric circles: from the nuclear circle of professed, vowed, and stable monks, including the seven martyrs, to a wider circle of the village community, mostly Muslim neighbors, to the more widely spread ecclesial community, not only in Tibhirine, but also in Fez, Algiers, and so many other cities where love for the Algerian people and their church were the biggest motivation.

This community in concentric circles became so because it is an ex-centric community. That is, a community that does not find its beginning, middle, and end in itself and in the lives of its core members, but which understands its life and vocation as a service to others. Even if it is a silent service, prayerful, without much stridency or visibility.

It is a community that exists out of itself, that lives out of itself, finding within itself the gifts and grace that should not be kept jealously but shared in generous solicitude to build, broaden, and strengthen communion. It is a community that points not to itself but to the communion of saints, a mystery for which the prior is especially devoted.[34] A community that is a cell of communion, that lives from and for communion and points to communion.

In the case of the Jesuits from the UCA of El Salvador, something similar takes place. The UCA community has a common mission, with very clear objectives: to give back wisdom and knowledge to transform the suffering Salvadoran reality. Inspired by the liberation theology that was then at its height on the Latin American continent, the UCA community is actually the description made by one of its exponents, the Peruvian priest Gustavo Gutiérrez.

It suggests a conception of community that fits in with the line of liberation theology defined and motivated by a common commitment, but developed in such a way as to allow debate and disagreement with tradition in terms of which commitment and its corresponding action are understood. Through the expressive understanding of action, Gustavo Gutiérrez develops a conception that justifies being a "community" of people sharing a common praxis, but bringing very different traditions to support this interpretation of praxis. The Peruvian theologian provides an argument from within his tradition to consider some types of collaboration with members of other traditions—whether one thinks of liberalism, Marxism, or other different religious traditions—as reflecting a fundamental choice and ultimately a community, not merely a matter of convenience or a short-term strategy.[35]

34. Cf. some writings where Christian of Chergé talks about the communion of the Saints. See Chergé, *L'invincible Esperance*; Salenson, *Christian de Chergé*; Salenson, *Prier 15 jours avec Christian de Chergé*.

35. Cf. what Thomas A. Lewis says about this, "Actions as the Ties That Bind," 562. The author states at the beginning of the section of his article that examines the conception of community for the Peruvian theologian that Gutiérrez's ecclesiology is profoundly modeled according to the conciliar documents *Lumen Gentium* and *Gaudium*

It is also worth mentioning Gutiérrez's statements in Medellín, stating that the present problem of the church is not so much about people who do not believe in God, but about people who do not practice their faith.[36] From there the Peruvian theologian argues that the integration of differences—different people, different perspectives, different traditions—will lead to an enrichment of praxis. Because our actions are a more authentic expression of our fundamental choice than our words, this plural and multiform unity of gestures and attitudes is definitely more significant than a unity based only on common professions of faith.[37]

Thus, the community led by the brilliant philosopher and thinker Ignacio Ellacuría was constantly opening new doors to dialogue, not only with ecclesial sectors, but with academics, civilians, and politicians. This dialogue enriched their positions, strengthened their community, and expanded the role of the university community beyond their campus, in the city, in the country, and in the world. And it reinforced the idea that not only did the Jesuit priests want an end to injustice and violence in El Salvador, but many other people, communities, instances—religious or not, ecclesial or not—supported the critical and utopian position of the dean and his community of Jesuit brothers and collaborators. And they expanded their strength and their historical and political repercussions.

Gutiérrez states that despite differences within such a group, the common praxis provides the necessary basis for meaningful and productive reflection on this praxis: "Only a sufficiently broad, rich, and intense revolutionary praxis, with the participation of people from different points of view, can create the conditions for a fruitful theory."[38] People, therefore, who embody and live the same fundamental orientation, even if they belong to different intellectual and religious traditions, will produce a common experience that provides the foundation for meaningful theoretical reflection together. One of Gutiérrez's fundamental concerns, especially at the beginning of his theological trajectory, is the dialogue between Marxists and Christians, fighting together in revolutionary times and situations. Without ever suggesting that Marxists will end up doing Christian theology and Christians becoming Marxists, he sees Christian eschatology transformed

---

et Spes. Applying to him the ecclesiology of models developed by Avery Dulles (*Models of the Church*) combines concepts of the church as communion, servant, and sacrament.

36. Gutiérrez, *Teología de la liberación*, 556.

37. Gutiérrez, *Teología de la liberación*, 557.

38. Gutiérrez, *Teología de la liberación*, 557.

as a result of contact between Christians and Marxists, who fight for a better world and live in coherence with it.[39]

Deep down is the distinction that was so dear to liberation theology, and which also prevailed in the aftermath of its peak. It is the difference between church and kingdom of God. No one fails to recall John Paul II's document talking about interreligious dialogue and criticizing the focus on the kingdom of some missionaries who did not bother to make explicit proclamation of the gospel, believing more in dialogue with people and respecting them in their differences.[40] Prior to this document, Latin American liberation theology, drinking from the new source of the conciliar documents, distinguished kingdom, world, and church. It thus emphasized the priority of the kingdom of God over the church, the community charged with carrying out and developing the kingdom project in the world.[41]

According to Leonardo Boff, "The Church is that part of the world which, in the power of the Spirit, has explicitly welcomed the kingdom in the person of Jesus Christ, the Son of God incarnate in oppression, who keeps the permanent memory and consciousness of the kingdom, celebrates its presence in the world and in itself and holds the grammar of its announcement in the service of the world."[42] The world is "the place of the historical realization of the kingdom." And the kingdom—"which encompasses the world and the church . . . is the good end of the totality of creation in God, finally liberated wholly from all imperfection and penetrated by the Divine who absolutely fulfills it."[43] Thus the kingdom is realized in the world and the church is its mediator—but not exclusive mediator, it is one of its signs, not the only sign.[44]

The monastic community of Tibhirine experienced and understood that the best way to fulfill their vocation as prayerful and contemplative was to be prayerful among prayerful people. And not only among Christians, but among other denominations, especially Islamic prayerful people. That was how they understood the fulfillment of the communion of saints that so inspired and attracted the mystical prior Christian de Chergé.

---

39. Gutiérrez, *Teología de la liberación*, 557.

40. *Redemptoris missio*, 1990, on the 25th anniversary of the Conciliar decree *Ad Gentes*.

41. L. Boff, *Igreja, carisma e poder*.

42. L. Boff, *Igreja, carisma e poder*, 16.

43. L. Boff, *Igreja, carisma e poder*, 16.

44. L. Boff, *Igreja, carisma e poder*, 84, 139.

That's why they paid a high price. Their freedom to move mystically and prophetically across the boundaries of differences was not welcomed by some. And although the poor, humble, Muslim people who knew and loved them welcomed and participated with open hearts in this pioneering evangelical experience, others—the radical terrorist groups or even the Algerian army and government—did not. And martyrdom and violent death were the price to pay.

The Jesuit community of UCA had a similar experience. Instead of self-understanding and self-building only as a theoretical academy that sees knowledge as an end in itself, they opened the academy and their mission from faith and religious consecration to other segments of society even if they did not share their reading of reality. UCA at that time led not only quality knowledge and cutting-edge education in the country and Central America, but it was leading a political process that wanted to liberate and seriously contribute to making new ways possible. It also paid the price for its visibility and its choice. As with the Tibhirine Trappists, martyrdom and violent death were the price to pay.

CHAPTER II

The Trappist Community
of Tibhirine

Algeria is earth and sun. Algeria is a cruel, yet beloved, suffering and passionate mother, hard and breastfeeding. More than in our temperate zones, it is proof of the mixture of good and evil, the inseparable dialectic of love and hate, the fusion of the opposites that constitute humanity.

—Albert Camus, *Le premier homme*

ALBERT CAMUS, THE FAMOUS French writer, carried his native Algeria in his blood and pen. He wrote about it and referenced it in one of his most distinguished novels.[1] We quote this great human rights thinker and supporter here to stress our claim that the Tibhirine community cannot be understood unless we glimpse their deep love for Algeria and specifically for Tibhirine and Mount Atlas, the place where the monastery was built and where the monks who occupy our reflection here—the community that was there with Christian de Chergé as prior in 1996—made their vows. The Notre Dame de l'Atlas monastery was known as a place of friendship between Muslims and Christians.[2] During four years, both the monastery and the neighboring village were spared the violence that ravaged the surrounding mountains. It is necessary to know something of the history and culture of that country before the kidnapping and murder of the monks, in order to realize the full extent of this fact and its repercussion in both local and universal society and the church.

With an area of 919,595 square miles, Algeria is the largest country in the Mediterranean basin and the largest in the entire African continent.

1. See Camus, *L'Étranger.*
2. Kiser, *Monks of Tibhirine,* 13.

It borders in the northeast with Tunisia, east with Libya, south with Niger and Mali, southwest with Mauritania and the contested territory of Western Sahara, and west with Morocco.

Algeria is a member of the United Nations (UN), the African Union (AU), and the Arab League almost right after independence in 1962, and has been a member of the Organization of Petroleum Exporting Countries (OPEC) since 1969. In February in 1989, Algeria participated, along with the other Maghreb states, in the process of creating the Arab Maghreb Union.

The Algerian Constitution defines "Islam, the Arabs and the Berbers" as "fundamental components" of the identity of the Algerian people, and the country as "the land of Islam, an integral part of the Great Maghreb, the Mediterranean and Africa."

Approximately 75 percent of Algerians use Berber languages (about 25 million) and over 85 percent use Arabic (about 28 million), both of which are official languages. Between 25 percent and 33 percent of the population speaks French (about 9–11 million inhabitants). In Algeria, Arabs typically use a local language variant, which differs in part from the classical Arabic language. Since independence, the governments of Algeria have sought to promote the expansion of Classical Arabic at the expense of local variants, and in contrast to French and Tamazight, the Algerian national language of Tuareg origin.

The language used within the Algerian political world is Arabic, while most use French for commerce and culture. Although not official, French is the second language of the country. The Tamazight language is often marginalized by the state, but as a result of Berber pressure it was finally recognized as a co-official language in Algeria.

As for religion, 99 percent of the population is Muslim and 1 percent is Catholic. There is a small Jewish minority who live mainly in Algiers. The rest of the large Jewish population prior to the creation of the state of Israel fled or was expelled after the country's independence.

Culturally, Algeria experienced a period of cultural splendor during the twelfth and thirteenth centuries, which coincided with the peak of Andalusian civilization. The Berber influence manifested itself above all in the field of literature, in which the poets al-Qalami (twelfth century) and Ibn al-Qafun stood out. Later it continued to cultivate the sciences and the studies of technology, history, and law, until, with the beginning of the French colonization in 1830, the Algerian culture progressively assimilated to the one of the metropolis, that is, of France. Arabic remained a literary language in the work of some native authors, such as playwrights Ksentini and Mahiedine, as well as poet Mohamed al-Id, and gained new impetus after independence, although French continued to be widely used.

The complexity of the country is also the secret of its fascination. And it was this mystery that fascinated many religious of French origin who went there to live their consecration in the Islamic milieu. Among them are many of the monks from the Notre Dame de l'Atlas community in Tibhirine. Although some were Algerian, most were French by birth and training. This is the case of Christian de Chergé, Brother Luc Dochier, Father Christophe Lebreton, Brother Michel Fleury, Father Bruno Lemarchand, Father Celestin Ringeard, and Brother Paul Favre Miville. Father Amedee was Algerian.[3]

Continuous Praise and Community Prayer

As a contemplative community, the one that was in Notre Dame de l'Atlas during the 1980s and 1990s is a prayer community in the first place—but an inculturated, situated, and committed prayer. We make this statement in social, geographical, and political terms, yes. But also, and this is no less important, in ecclesial terms. These monks formed a contemplative community in an Islamic country, and this had consequences for the way they organized the monastery, daily life, and even prayers. And in a definite way, even their destiny and death.

As Argentine Father Bernardo Olivera, the general abbot of the order at the time, said on the occasion of the martyrdom of the monks, "What united them was their search for God in community, their love for the Algerian people and a link of unwavering fidelity to the pilgrim Church of Algeria."[4] This was an important element for all members of that community, but most especially for Christian de Chergé, who was previously a diocesan priest in Paris and chose to become a monk in this particular Algerian monastery, obeying a call from God to be a "prayerful person among other prayerful people" (in French, *priant parmi les priants*).[5] And for him, the "other" prayerful with whom he raised his own personal prayer to God was not only constituted and personified by his brother monks, but also,

3. Olivera, *How Far to Follow*, 6–9.

4. Olivera, *How Far to Follow*, 10.

5. Henning, *Christian de Chergé*.

very strongly and in a very special way, by the Islamic people who lived there in the community in which they were inserted.

Historian John Kiser, author of an important book on the events of Tibhirine, states: "The monks were not martyrs for their faith. They did not die because they were Christians. They died because they did not want to leave their Muslim friends, who depended on them and who lived in equal danger."[6] We allow ourselves here to disagree partly with the historian, while acknowledging the importance of the book he has written on the subject. From the theological point of view, we believe that yes, the monks died for their faith. Not in the traditional view that they were killed for "hatred of the faith" (*odium fidei*, once considered the only cause for martyrdom to be recognized).[7] However, in Christian terms there is no faith that does not work for charity. The refusal to leave where they were despite the danger, leaving to seek security, or leaving the community for which they felt responsible and which was experiencing insecurity and threat as their own, is an act not only of bravery and courage but of charity in the most proper sense of the term. In their case, this act and decision finds its origin and inspiration in their faith. It is not only a political decision, but also spiritual and theological. Although we may consider and even state that this decision had strong political repercussions.[8]

In this sense, although it cannot be said that the monks were murdered out of hatred of the Christian and Catholic faith, it can be said, in our view, that the reason for their murder and violent death was the fact that they wished and decided to stand strong until the end in the consistent commitment with their Christian faith and the Gospel of Jesus. That's why they were killed. It should not be ignored that in the statement the Groupe Islamique Armé (GIA) sent announcing their execution said that they were killed because they proselytized, e.g., were not locked up in

6. Kiser, *Monks of Tibhirine*, 13.

7. Cf. Catechism of the Catholic Church, n. 957, 1173, 2113, 2472, and particularly n. 2473. Martyrdom is the supreme witness given to the truth of the faith: it means bearing witness even unto death. The martyr bears witness to Christ who died and rose, to whom he is united by charity. He bears witness to the truth of the faith and of Christian doctrine. He endures death through an act of fortitude. "Let me become the food of the beasts, through whom it will be given me to reach God" (Ign. *Rom.* 4).

8. Cf. Father Armand Veilleux OCSO's magnificent text on the political implications before and after the disappearance of the monks, leading to the present day to suspect that they were not killed by the radical Islamists but by the Algerian army. Father Veilleux's text is April 9, 1996, when the monks were still missing and news of their death had not yet been received. In Veilleux, "Padres do Deserto."

their monastery, but had contact with Muslims and could attract them to the faith being radically repudiated by Islam.[9] Subsequently, the conjectures about the actual circumstances of the monks' murder will relativize the allegations of this statement.

With all these features, however, there is no doubt that the Tibhirine community was a praying community. The general abbot himself, Dom Bernardo Olivera, was impressed when he met the two survivors after the community attack that resulted in the abduction and death of the seven monks.[10] Amedee and Jean Pierre, who escaped alive, met with the general abbot to read the testimony of a priest who was invited to stay at the monastery on the same night of the abduction. He writes that when the overnight guests discovered that the GIA had taken seven monks and that only Amedee and Jean Pierre were there, it was late at night. They then decided to go to bed to wait until dawn so that they could go by daylight to the city. But Amedee replied, "I haven't finished my rosary." The others then finished the rosary with him and only then went to bed.[11] This small and moving detail shows us how prayer—even the simplest devotion, such as the rosary—was the air the monks breathed.

This short story reaffirms our conviction that prayer is an essential source for monks, a reserve, a pillar. Like the prior himself, Christian de Chergé says, "At night we take the Book, when others take the guns."[12] And prayer—as this Christian spiritual master also masters—has no practical or visible purpose. It is absolutely free. There is no intention for the monks in praying that leads to a practical consequence, such as: we pray to be stronger, to be more fed, etc.[13] Prayer is free and gratuitous. As Christian says: "We

9. Henning, *Petite vie des moines de Tibhirine*, 72.

10. Christian, Paul, Christophe, Michel, Luc, Célestin, and Bruno.

11. Olivera, *How Far to Follow*, 97.

12. Chenu, *Sept vies pour Dieu*, 253.

13. We can see here a great coincidence of the monks' prayer and the way they conceive and live it with the thought of some contemporary theologians. In particular, the Galician theologian Andres Torres Queiruga, who most thought and wrote about this, radically questions the prayer of petition, supporting its claims in Scripture and in the ecclesial theological tradition. It is he who says: "When we cut the flow of the petition, we must be aware that our being is always accompanied by God, energized, liberated for the proper human task: it is not a matter of 'asking' us to help, but to believe in your already real help, despite all possible obscurity. In addition, we are opening ourselves to its impulse in the adult responsibility of those who know that everything is already surrendered to their freedom (which, however, is not alone . . .)." In Queiruga, "Para além da oração de petição."

pray to find the Beloved."[14] And in this statement one can already see not only the charism of the monks that shapes their praying life but also undoubtedly recognize the great mystic that is the prior of Tibhirine.

The Constitutions of the Order describe the spiritual journey the monk is invited to take throughout his life:

> By the word of God, monks are formed to a mastery of the heart and action that will allow them, obeying the Spirit, to reach the purity of heart and the unceasing memory of God's presence. . . . The monks follow in the footsteps of all those who in the past centuries have been called by God to spiritual combat in the desert. As Citizens of Heaven, they will convert into strangers to worldly style. They renounce themselves to follow Christ. Through humility and obedience they fight against the pride and rebellion of sin. In simplicity and hard work they are looking for the promised bliss to the poor. For their zealous hospitality they share Christ's peace and hope with those who, like them, are walking. . . . The monastery is a picture of the mystery of the Church.[15]

After the Second Vatican Council, however, many of the Catholic contemplative orders reread their constitutions with another eye, in the spirit of that new springtime of the church. These institutes of contemplative consecrated life understood that their unceasing prayer and praise should take place in a situation of rooting in the modern world marked by secularization.[16] Moreover, the church recognized that it was situated in a context of great spiritual upheaval and a hitherto unnoticed pluralism. An openness to diversity began to take place, not only religious but of various dimensions: cultural, scientific, sexual.[17] This is still the case today, perhaps in an even more challenging and complex way. And among the present diversity, religious diversity stands out.

In this way, many monasteries began to become deeply aware of being called to a prayer ministry not only in the cloister, but situated in the midst of the church with a conscious openness to the world.[18] In addition,

---

14. Ray, *Christian de Chergé*, 83.

15. "Constitutions of the Trappist Order."

16. Proving this, we see the examples of René Voillaume, Madeleine Delbrel, Père Caffarel, Thomas Merton, etc.

17. Charles de Foucauld pioneered this Christian presence alongside another religion. His life took place in Algeria. Therefore, although living before the council, he embodies as few his spirit.

18. We cite here the example of Thomas Merton, the remarkable American Trappist

many contemplatives were called to be always in prayer, among others who also pray but belong to other religious traditions. It was a matter of living the Christian contemplative vocation in the midst of the differences by which humanity is composed. There began to be born a monasticism open to interreligious dialogue, in the spirit of the document *Nostra Aetate*, which recognizes the legitimacy and positivity of other religions, even non-Christian ones. Thus, their life, besides being a permanently prayerful life, also implies extending this praying vocation to other prayers belonging to other traditions. This becomes especially important in a world where historical Christianity no longer has the hegemony once enjoyed, and where the great religious traditions coexist geographically and spiritually. In such a shaped world, too, embryos of new spiritual syntheses emerge that no longer allow us to see the religious potential of humanity in terms of a univocal belonging: the Christian and above all Catholic ecclesiastical. Within this framework, contemplative religious orders are called to pray and learn to pray in mixed communities where Christians and non-Christians seek together the experience of God and an intense and deep spiritual life. These orders or communities began to be more strongly and explicitly present even in non-Christian countries, and even in places that showed hostility to Christianity.

Nevertheless, there is another element that characterizes the prayer life of the monks of Tibhirine: the monk's prayer, in the cenobytic model, is not solitary but communal. The Trappist community is a community of prayer and the community is the praying subject who lives the spirituality and mysticism, rather than the individual. This is the case with every religious vocation and every monastic vocation.[19] In this way, the process experienced by the community of Notre Dame de l'Atlas, the monastery—after struggling to leave Paris and leaving a brilliant career in the parish of Montmartre—brought Christian de Chergé to balance. This urgency was due to the appeal

who, in his Louisville enlightenment, felt called to love concretely all those whom he saw enlightened by the grace of God. He did so by writing, participating in issues and political struggles of his time, and in dialogue with philosophy and oriental monarchism. About Merton, see the beautiful thesis of Pereira, "A Contemplação Como Resposta em Thomas Merton," among many others. See Thomas Merton's extensive bibliography in Merton, "Thomas Merton's Life and Work." See also the list of his publications online, with digital access to several of them in Merton, "Internet Bibliography."

19. There is one exception in the field of non-cenobite monastic religious life: the hermitic vocation. A hermit is one who, called by God, chooses to live in solitude, in a life of prayer and penance. Hermit vocations are rare and the most common are monastic vocations.

of the times and the renewal of the church and also the arrival of its new member. Christian was far more aware of this than the other members of the community and was vividly mobilized by the novelty of a contemplative life in a different culture. But he could not walk alone. He had to pass this on to his brothers in order not to betray his calling.

At times he painfully feels these differences within the community:

> There is a certain presence in the world, which must configure our monasteries as havens for prayer, but this "opening" path is somehow terribly demanding and we often believe that we are called to "go out" rather than "let in" . . . what we are asked to do is to be men of prayer, to be nothing more than that. And it is this evidence that, thus giving me a very long-term goal is undoubtedly enough to savor the peace that is only to be expected from Jesus, which is known to be found in no society, no environment, no monasticism. Once this connection is well established, environment and community become essential as daily revealing of our own inadequacies, and we discover within ourselves all the components of that lukewarmness we talk about, deploring it for affecting all monastic structures so much.[20]

The monks of Tibhirine were then somehow "compelled" to learn to pray together, not only in the liturgy of ordinary times of prayer. But they had to do a much deeper learning: to be a body in prayer, icon of the mystery of the church, praying together in communion of heart and mind. But equally and in a constitutive way, to pray for openness to the Muslim tradition within which they lived. And especially for the community where they chose to live and pronounce their vows, this profound learning of prayer prepared them for the situation they would have to live through: insecurity, violence, persecution, and martyrial death.

We see that the discernment process they lived together would not be possible without a profound experience of prayer. Through prayer, unceasing and communal, they really became a pleasing offering to God, completely given to him, all expectant of him, and praying also for others, even the enemies who threatened them. In the document written by the community on the rereading of the order's charism in the situation in which they lived, prayer has a prominent place. There appears the so-called sense of greater surrender to God and prayer of intercession.[21]

20. Ray, *Christian de Chergé*, 85.
21. Chenu, *Sept vies pour Dieu*, 181.

There also appears the confession of one of the monks: "My prayer? What about it? . . . but there is the prayer of Jesus. And his silence when 'his mouth takes over the sky'! . . . It seems to me that here I have received thanksgiving, praise, perhaps also worship." And yet: "Certain elements of our regularity find there a recovery of meaning and intensity: the priority of a life in faith, privileging the night . . . the psalms, the office, and often the readings of the Eucharist."[22]

Ora et Labora in an Islamic Country

The main rule created by the Benedictine monasteries of the Middle Ages was as follows: "Ora et labora." This Latin phrase means "pray and work." It marks an important step in the way of conceiving not only the life of faith, but the human life as a whole. In the Greek world, physical labor was considered slave occupation. The truly free human being is devoted exclusively to spiritual realities, physical work being somewhat inferior, left to people who were not capable of this higher spiritual existence. In Acts 11:19–26 we find the moment when the disciples were first called Christians. The New Testament text states that they prayed in the temple but also worked, teaching the word everywhere and at all times. The binomial "prayer-work" is therefore constitutive of the Christian life from an early age. Benedict of Nursia takes this up again and sets the lifestyle he founded.

In Christian mysticism, the phrase "prayer and work" (or in Latin, *ora et labora*) thus refers to the monastic practice of working and praying, generally associated with its use in the Rule of St. Benedict.[23] Benedict of Nursia saw prayer and work as inseparable partners, and believed in the combination of contemplation with action.[24] The phrase expresses the need to balance prayer and work in monastic environments and has been used in many religious communities from the Middle Ages thereafter.[25] Anyway, the expression was popularized by St. Benedict in the fifth century and to this day identifies the monastic way of life in Western Christianity.

---

22. Chenu, *Sept vies pour Dieu*, 181–82.

23. Grün, *Benedict of Nursia*.

24. Pratt and Homan, *Benedict's Way*.

25. However, it cannot be forgotten that this expression was also present in Judaism. For example, the motto of the religious Zionist organization Bnei Akiva is "Torah and work" (Torah v'avodah).

Some orders (such as the Cistercian) applied the concept directly to agricultural work and this became an element of the land reclamation movement of the process of destruction itself of agricultural development in Western Europe. This is the case with the Tibhirine community.

When Christian de Chergé arrives at the monastery of Notre Dame de l'Atlas, the community does not have a homogeneous and unified view of the meaning of its presence in Algeria. The reasons why each of the monks live in that country are as diverse as the monks themselves. They were: attention to the sick (Brother Lucas), spiritual service to Christians living in Algeria, monastic life in Africa, affective attachment to the country, very simple monastic reality, a more humble life, etc.

Christian, however, had a very clear notion of having chosen Algeria with one mission in mind: to live a spiritual presence in the Muslim milieu. And he considers this to be compatible with the founder's motto: "Ora et labora." It was never quite understood by his brothers, nor by the superiors of the order. And he suffered greatly because his monastic vocation was not understood as an authentic apostolic vocation.[26] However, he was convinced, especially after spending two years in Rome studying Arabic, that the Spirit works more comfortably from the grassroots. He writes to his friends, "It is necessary that the fire burns, the fire of which Jesus thirsted."[27] And because of that, he postulates his integration into the Algerian monastery.

But by the time he arrives at the Trappist novitiate in 1971, he has to learn to refrain from his impatience and haste. To exercise the virtue of patience that he lacks, there is nothing better than manual labor in apiaries, in the oil mill, or in the care of lavender. And he testifies to this, writing to a monk friend: "It is a very exceptional joy to be able to indulge in such boring and monotonous work . . . having the spirit released by a verse of St. John (the best companion, the one of the direct contact, the Christ)."[28]

Slowly and steadily, the Tibhirine community began to have a very clear and profound awareness that prayer and work must be lived together. For example, Father Christophe Lebreton says he loves to pray in the places where he works: "at work, in the workshop, near a tree. . . . I would love to be able to say my prayer there, in the midst of things, with world and my existence being enlarged, transfigured."[29] Being also an inspired

---

26. Ray, *Christian de Chergé*, 80.

27. Ray, *Christian de Chergé*, 81.

28. Ray, *Christian de Chergé*, 91.

29. Lebreton, *Aime jusqu' au bout du feu*, 76.

and tireless writer, he has notes, poems, and beautiful written texts. He says in his writings, "Writing is the wound of a sick man" and sets himself a daily task: "To transcribe the gift each day."[30] Christophe then discovers in writing his integrated means of prayer.[31]

There are also many testimonies of Brother Luc Dochier, who, as a doctor, aided more than one hundred patients each day with love and devotion, caring for them and helping the parents to raise and educate children. At 82 years old, the "toubib"[32] took care of everyone for over forty years without demanding anything else in return. Sometimes discouraged by so much misery and hard work, he remembered his meeting with Marthe Robin,[33] in the 1950s, who promised he would never run out of medicines. Always on duty, he welcomed all demands: "A sick person is neither a soldier nor a 'maquisard.' He is a sick person,"[34] he said, stressing that he always treated everyone without asking for their identity or requesting anything in return.

It is not only the work inside the monastery, however, that marks the Tibhirine community, but also the fact that it is a prayerful and active presence, open to people living in the neighborhood, forming an expanded community with them. For Christian, it is very clear what his vocation is: to listen to the spirituality of Islam, to share the spiritual life with them, to be a prayerful person among other prayerful people.[35]

What gives each and every community the strength to fight to live the monastic ideal of prayer and work is the community itself. As Christian writes to his monk friend: "and at the end of the day, the little miracle is this instability (four of us stabilized against eleven), where every morning the community perpetuates itself."[36]

This is why—by this somewhat original way of understanding things—some monks doubted Christian de Chergé's monastic vocation, seeing him

30. Henning, *Petite vie des moines de Tibhirine*, 24–25.

31. Palumbo and Bertolini, *La casa en el Puente*.

32. Toubib, Arabic word for doctor, medic.

33. Marthe Robin was a simple peasant girl from the Lyon region of France, who attended more than 100,000 people in her room where she was bedridden until her death on February 6, 1981, seriously ill for over fifty years. Brother Luc was one of many who came to visit her on his bed of pain.

34. This was the name of the Resistants, or members of the Resistance, a clandestine movement that aimed to sabotage the advance of German Nazi troops. On Brother Luc Dochier's attitude about his medical work, see "Irmão Luc."

35. Henning, *Petite vie des moines de Tibhirine*, 24–25.

36. Henning, *Petite vie des moines de Tibhirine*, 93.

a little too active, wondering if he would better serve the church as a priest in the diocese of Oran. They did not understand his insistence on learning Arabic. They asked themselves, "Aren't monks men of silence? Why learn another language?" Nor was his interest in Islamic spirituality understood by anyone.[37] But surely the whole community came a long way in the dialogue with Islam thanks to the prior's firm convictions. And that strongly influenced the direction that community would later undertake.

A Contemplative Community in Dialogue with Another Religion

The difficulty for religions to coexist peacefully, living in dialogue with each other, is historic. As Julien Green asks in anguish: "When will religions finally become unity between people and no more additional reasons to exterminate each other?"[38] We believe the experience of the Tibhirine monks can bring a powerful light to this question and give it a differentiated quality of perspective and growth.

Christian de Chergé felt a call from God to be a prayerful person among prayerful people, and among these prayer companions he always included his Muslim brothers and sisters. His vocation was to follow a "particular Christian monastic vocation in the Muslim world," as his biographer Marie Christine Ray summarizes.[39] But he was neither the first nor the only one to feel and think in that direction and to experience and carry out very special Islamic-Christian dialogue. Among the prior readings are, for example, the writings of Max Thurian, Taizé's brother and pioneer of an ecumenical monastery that attracts a large number of young people each year and already has foundations around the world.[40] And Max Thurian says: "It is important for the Church to ensure, in addition to what Islam already does, a fraternal

37. Ray, *Christian de Chergé*, 94.

38. Green, *La lumière du monde*, 99.

39. Ray, *Christian de Chergé*, 150.

40. The Taizé Community is a Christian ecumenical community located in Taizé, Burgundy, France. It was founded in 1940 by Brother Roger, who remained his prior until his death on August 16, 2005, and is dedicated to reconciliation. The ecumenical community is made up of over one hundred men of various nationalities, representing Protestant and Catholic denominations. Community life is centered on prayer and Christian meditation. Young people from around the world visit Taizé every week to integrate into community life.

presence of men and women who share the lives of Muslims as closely as possible, in silence, prayer and friendship."[41]

Before him, Charles de Foucauld[42]—mentioned previously as well—was a true pioneer of prayerful insertion among Muslims. After going to the Trappists and doing other experiments such as living in Nazareth and being a carpenter, like Jesus, he went to live alone as a hermit in Tamanrassett in the middle of the desert. There he lived his splendid spirituality, where the Eucharist had a central place. He was killed by Tuaregs passing by.

Also Louis Massignon, a Catholic scholar of Islam and one of the pioneers of the Catholic-Muslim mutual endeavor, stands out among these advocates of dialogue. He was the only influential figure of the twentieth century who defended and lived a relationship of the Catholic Church with Islam. He concentrated ever more deeply on reading and reflecting on the work of Mohandas K. Gandhi, whom he considered a saint. He is responsible among Catholics for the designation of Islam as an Abrahamic faith.[43] There is a growing consensus among scholars that their relentless research, esteem for Islam and Muslims, and the accompanying of highly skilled students in Islamic studies have largely paved the way for the positive vision of Islam articulated in the dogmatic constitutions *Lumen Gentium* and the declaration *Nostra Aetate* from the Second Vatican Council.[44] Although he himself was a Catholic, he tried to understand Islam from within, and thus exerted great influence on the way in which Islam was viewed in the West. Among other things, it paved the way for greater openness within the Catholic Church toward Islam as documented in the pastoral declaration *Nostra Aetate*.[45] All these influences marked the Tibhirine community very concretely through its prior, voracious reader of the entire bibliography on this subject.

What is very special about Christian de Chergé and his community is exactly the community characteristic. Unlike the examples we cited earlier—Charles de Foucauld, Louis Massignon—this is not an individual who decides to approach Islam and enter into dialogue with it. We are not facing an individual spiritual itinerary, as could be the ones mentioned earlier. It is a whole Christian and Catholic community inserted in a place of Islamic

41. Thurian, *Tradition et renouveau*, 14.

42. 1858–1916.

43. Geffré, "La portee theologique," 9.

44. Krokus, *Theology of Louis.*

45. *Nostra Aetate*, n. 3.

predominance as a guest rather than a dominant presence. From a poor and begging position, they ask for the grace of dialogue with their brothers and sisters of Islam. And for that they pray with them.[46]

Due to the strength of community ties, the monks of Tibhirine risked bold gestures. For example, Muslims in the vicinity of the monastery had no place to pray. In 1988, the monks gave them a large room that was not in use. Speakers were set in a tree very close by. From then on, the monastery bells and the call of the muezzin would alternate in order to call Christians and Muslims to prayer respectively according to the time of day.[47]

This community has tried to understand itself as consisting of monks who are both sentinels and watchmen. They find their theological matrix in biblical texts such as the prophet Isaiah, who asks, "Watchman, how much longer the night?"[48] This feeling of being vigilant sentinels grew after the terrorist group visit on Christmas Eve. Once the first reaction to this visit passed, the monks asked around for advice and tried to find meaning in leaving without hope of returning. Then the call to be watchful sentinels, ensuring that the peace and life of this human and Muslim community grew, eventually overcame. So they gave up leaving, exposing themselves to the same risk of other religious and lay people living there, as well as the entire surrounding community.

Father Christophe Lebreton affirms: "We would like to remain here as monks, men of peace and prayer . . . and work."[49] And also Christian de Chergé, who feels that the Quran also calls for dialogue, says: "People of the Book! Come to a common word between us and you" (3,64). Therefore, after getting ever closer to their brothers and sisters of Islam, they will create with others the "Lien de paix" (Peace link) movement, Rkibat in Arabic, which continued to exist after his death. The purpose of the movement was the mysticism of the encounter. As Father Christophe Lebreton attests: "Do you know what prayer unites the members of Rkibat? 'Lord, set us up for the meeting!'"[50]

---

46. Cf. the text "Nuit de feu," written by Chergé, in *L'Invincible espérance*. Texts new and present by Chergé, *L'Invincible espérance*, 33–38, which we reproduced, translated by ourselves, in this chapter.

47. Henning, *Petite vie des moines de Tibhirine*, 37.

48. Isa 21:11.

49. Kiser, *Passion pour l'Algerie*, 309.

50. Henning, *Petite vie des moines de Tibhirine*, 97–99.

All this shows that the monks were very aware of what the Abbot General, Dom Bernardo Olivera, says about being monks in an Islamic country: "Being monks every day, we are martyrs every day. Keeping a high testimony on daily life requires more courage and bravery than to witness at once through a supreme act, no matter how supreme."[51] And the whole community lived that ideal.

But if, on the one hand, their harmony and coexistence with the people of the neighboring community was growing and deepening, on the other hand, the terrorist groups saw in that community a good target to obtain some elements they wanted. First, they approached the monastery for money, resources, and Brother Lucas's medical services. He attended and treated them at the monastery, but not outside, in obedience to the prior who would not let him go to the mountain with the GIA guerrillas.[52]

The radical Islamist groups did not welcome the popularity of the monks among their neighbors, nor the fact that some (very few) people asked for baptism and approached Christianity. The GIA (Groupe Islamique Armé) statement sent on April 16 following the kidnapping of the monks explicitly states: "God has commanded believers to kill unbelievers, starting with those closest to them and those who are the most dangerous and harmful to the religion and life of Muslims. . . . These prisoner monks live with people and lead them astray from the divine path, urging them to evangelize."[53]

In any case, the feelings of the Trappist community were not to hate those who hated them but to forgive them with the same feeling of forgiveness that Jesus preached in the Sermon on the Mount and practiced during his life and death. As Father Christophe says: never separate from Jesus, but accept death without accepting what causes the hatred of those who killed. It is a delicate and complex subject, no doubt. In the end Christophe himself asks, "But should I accept the death of my brothers?"[54]

---

51. Henning, *Petite vie des moines de Tibhirine*, 93.

52. Cf. above all the text of Father Armand Veilleux, quoted above, which states that Brother Lucas did not go to the mountain to treat the jihadist leader who led the group that came to the monastery for the prudence and recommendation of the prior.

53. Henning, *Petite vie des moines de Tibhirine*, 72.

54. Olivera, *How Far to Follow*, 63.

The True Spirit of the Community of Tibhirine: Service, Peace, and Discernment

The monks of Tibhirine were a community deeply sensitive to all the problems surrounding them. For example, they were very much connected by feelings of true friendship—and not solely or mainly by pastoral or proselytizing interests—to the monastery's neighbors, a very poor community, lacking in many things.

Despite the situation that some of them might have had before entering monastic life—Christian belonged to a well-off family, Christophe was also from an upper-middle-class family—they entered monastic life to truly live in poverty. Dom Bernardo, the abbot general, says of Father Christophe: "He was a tireless writer, an enthusiastic guitarist, a poet of the heart, always with the poor and the marginalized."[55] They lived their daily lives in search of ever-greater radical poverty, integrating spiritual and material poverty. They were very close to the members of the community surrounding the monastery, which was mostly Muslim poor. Brother Lucas was tireless in caring for them, very devoted in his medical service to those who could not afford to seek adequate medical care.

About Brother Michel, Dom Bernardo says that he was a man of few words, a silent worker. On Father Celestin, he says that, as a former diocesan priest, he exercised his pastoral ministry with the marginals, prostitutes, and homosexuals of Nantes, his hometown.[56] And he continued to exercise his relationships with the community around the monastery with extreme sensitivity, compassion, and simplicity. Father Paul was skilled in all kinds of manual work and was responsible for the irrigation system in the monastery garden.[57]

It can be seen from this that a poor *community* is very close to another poor community, of which it is a constitutive part and for which it has a deep love. In return, they are thus well considered by the same neighboring community. Christian said one day to people in the neighborhood where they lived: "We are in solidarity with the Algerians like the bird on the branch." And one young man replied, "You are the branch and we are the birds. If you leave, where will we go?"[58] For them, solidarity

55. Olivera, *How Far to Follow*, 7.

56. Olivera, *How Far to Follow*, 9

57. Olivera, *How Far to Follow*, 7–13.

58. Olivera, *How Far to Follow*, 97; Henning, *Petite vie des moines de Tibhirine*, 52–53.

and service to the poor means something very serious and is an important part of their commitment, their source of strength and joy. This neighboring community was therefore an important element in their discernment to leave or to remain when violence began to grow and become more threatening in the vicinity of where they lived.

They are also a *peace community.* The decision not to accept military protection after the GIA visit on Christmas Eve was communal and the subject of a community vote.[59] It was decided in a community discernment and firmly asserted by Christian before the mayor and the army beyond the Archbishop of Algiers. It was a commitment of absolute nonviolence.

Brother Jean Pierre—one of the two survivors of the murder—when he tells the story of recent times to his brothers, states: "the choice to be unarmed and without protection from any security and armed measures, or to flee to the city, was made early in the process, as it was a shared decision to follow the Gospel 'as lambs among wolves,' our only weapons being faithfulness in charity and faith in the power of the Holy Spirit working in human hearts. This faith also rested in the goodwill of people we hoped would see the trust we placed in them, remaining unarmed, in their hands and in such a dangerous place."[60]

Christian will also comment on this in December 1995: "We needed to be firm in our refusal to let either of us identify with one camp or another, to remain free in order to peacefully contest weapons and the means of violence and exclusion. To remain what we are in this context and to proclaim concretely a Gospel of love for all that that respect for difference implies.[61]

The fact is that after the kidnapping and death of the monks, there were no witnesses that night—Amedee and Jean Pierre saw only from afar from their rooms and heard nothing—to tell the details of the violence in the monastery. But there is a state of mind, an attitude resulting from a search, that certainly dominated the community. If we recall the unceasing prayer of Prior Christian de Chergé during the last months: "Lord, disarm me, disarm them," we can imagine how this simple and ardent prayer may have mobilized the hearts of the kidnapped monks.[62]

59. Olivera, *How Far to Follow,* 18.

60. Olivera, *How Far to Follow,* 75.

61. Henning, *Petite vie des moines de Tibhirine,* 10.

62. Henning, *Petite vie des moines de Tibhirine,* 61.

About this extraordinary example of evangelical meekness, Jean Marie Rouart—a scholar, writer, and brilliant French intellectual—stated before the Académie Française: "They had one more uniqueness, alongside that of being between two fires, two violences, two intolerances. Not only did they not carry weapons to defend themselves, but they responded to violence with meekness, to offense with forgiveness."[63]

Finally, it is a community of *men of spirit and prayer*, and from this prayer a community discernment emerges. Especially in times of adversity, when violence is real and the threat that knocks on the door is very real, they examine the situation in peace, seeing the real possibility of martyrdom. But instead of despairing or becoming anxious, they remain in a peaceful expectation that God will manifest his will.

There are beautiful testimonies about this, such as that of Father Christophe, who was very devoted to the Virgin Mary and made a special consecration of his life to her. He writes in his diary: "Near you (Mary), I am what I should be: oblation." And he goes on, reflecting with great clarity on the possibility of martyrdom, commenting on what the mayor told him, that staying would be a collective suicide: "The martyr is not a kamikaze or a suicide. We reaffirm our reasons for staying. We see that we are at the junction between two clashing groups here and, to some extent, everywhere in the West and the Middle East."[64]

As the poet he is, he expressed with moving and beautiful words the situation: "We are in a situation of epiclesis."[65] This is how they are, and even more so this is how they feel they must wait for God to consume their consecration, which may be through martyrdom and death. Christophe goes on along the same lines: "I am learning what it means for the Church. I see you adorned like a bride to your Suffering Servant."[66] His poetic sensibility sees martyrdom as a liturgy.[67]

---

63. Henning, *Petite vie des moines de Tibhirine*, 86.

64. Olivera, *How Far to Follow*, 55.

65. According to Christian theology, "epiclese" (from ancient Greek: ἐπίκλησις—epíklesis) is a fusion of the words *epí* and *kaléō*: "to call upon." This is the invocation prayer that asks the descent of the Holy Spirit into the sacraments. It is especially important and fundamental in the mass, taking place after the chant of the holy, in which the priest asks the Holy Spirit to descend upon the community and the offerings of bread and wine. I have several canons and instructions on the necessity and means of applying the epiclese. Regarding this, more complete information can be found in "Epiclese."

66. Olivera, *How Far to Follow*, 55.

67. Young, "Père Marquette Lectures."

Dom Bernardo Olivera will gather more writings from Christophe during those terrible days. They are full of theology about the configuration of their community: "Beside this, there is something unique about our way of being Church, how we react to facts, how we expect them and live them in practice. It has to do with a certain awareness that we are responsible not for doing something, but for being something in response to Truth and Love. I see something about our particular way of being, which is being cenobitic monks. Resist change. And move forward."[68] And he compares what it says with the Psalms where words speak of remaining and resisting change.

Christophe views his death and that of his community as a service. He writes, "The night I offered in your name the infinite service of saying to myself, 'I forgive you.' And that means I know my body is for you and you for my body? I cannot say if I am united with you. I only choke up and beg never to be separated from you, the temple of your Spirit, which comes to me from the Father and is given by you. I do not belong. Mary is in me a guarantee of this renunciation that was total and radical in her. Close to her, I am. Then I will be able to glorify you with my body."[69]

Like Christophe Lebreton, poet and gifted with great spiritual sensitivity, Christian de Chergé will also read his facts about life. For him, it was not just a matter of living the experience that was presented, but of driving all the discernment of his community toward the will of God.

Christian de Chergé: Prior, Mystic, and Martyr

Christian de Chergé was born in Colmar, Alsace, in a large, aristocratic, and well-educated family. His father was a military man who had passed the Saint Cyr School[70] and the family lived in Algeria for a while because Lieutenant Guy de Chergé, Christian's father, was transferred there. The eldest son, who was always very religious and very close to his mother, who was a very devout Catholic, felt the vocation to be a priest from an early age and entered the seminary of the diocese of Paris. During his formation process, he was sent as an officer to Algeria in the midst of the war. Two figures attracted him in his childhood and adolescence, close to

68. Olivera, *How Far to Follow*, 59.

69. Olivera, *How Far to Follow*, 63.

70. Saint Cyr is a famous French military college of higher education that trains infantry officers and a part of the national guard officers. See "Escola Militar."

Islam. The first was his mother, who, seeing him watching the prostrate Muslims in prayer, said to him, "They pray to God, we cannot mock it. They also worship God." Commenting on this fact years later, Christian says, "Ever since then, I've known that the God of Islam and the God of Jesus Christ make no number."[71]

The other is Mohammed, a godly Muslim and father of ten children. As a seminarian and military man, Christian had a strong experience meeting this man, who was a country guard. Mohammed knew that he was exposed to the radicalisms reigning in that circumstance of war, being close and friendly to a Frenchman. They talked a lot about the differences between Christianity and Islam. Mohammed knew he was being threatened in the violent situation the country was going through during those times. And he asked Christian to pray for him, even if, according to him, "Christians don't know how to pray."[72] "I received this criticism as a reproach to a church that does not present itself as a prayer community," says Christian.[73] During a confrontation with radical Muslims, Mohammed intervened in favor of Christian. The next day they found him dead, beheaded. For Christian, this was the greatest proof of love: giving one's life for the other.[74] He knew that solidarity with his own person had been the cause of Mohammed's murder, and this eucharistic gift impressed him so much that it accompanied him throughout his life.

The person, the existence of Christian de Chergé, was profoundly transformed because of this encounter and testimony. He writes years later about this friend, saying, "This whole confusing period has been struck by a ray of light, which has changed my way of illuminating the understanding of my life and brought me to where I am."[75] Christian never forgot this prayerful Muslim friend and included him in the communion of saints,[76] which surpasses the boundaries of religions. It was a founding experience in his process of vocational discernment toward a positive relationship with the Muslim faith, which he called "pilgrimage toward the communion of saints, where Christians and Muslims share the same

71. Ray, *Christian de Chergé*, 21.

72. Ray, *Christian de Chergé*, 48.

73. Ray, *Christian de Chergé*, 48; Henning, *Petite vie des moines de Tibhirine*, 89.

74. Ray, *Christian de Chergé*, 48.

75. Ray, *Christian de Chergé*, 47.

76. On how the prior conceived the communion of saints, cf. Salenson, *Prier 15 jours avec Christian de Chergé*, 1; Salenson, *Christian de Chargé*, 80–81.

joy of being children.[77] He feels the call to monastic life, but firmly linked to Islam and Algeria. Dialogue with Islam is now a constitutive part of his monastic vocation.[78] And he recognizes in the Eucharistic gift of Mohammed's life the gift of Christ himself.[79]

When you feel the call to be a monk and enter the Cistercian order, you also feel the need to unite with others and sustain your prayer within this praying community. He knows his own fragility and suspects his absolute and radical temperament. The community will be a protection against the risk of being a sniper in its own way. He also believes that the presence of Christian monks, whose visible prayer seven times a day resembles the ritual prayer of Muslims, opens the door to a true encounter with the praying people of Islam. His vocation calls not so much to deepen only in Christian prayer, but to unite and "confuse" it with that of Muslim believers.[80]

When he enters the Tibhirine monastery, he brings along all his previous experiences and desires. Engaging in contemplative life in Algeria, he imposes on himself a double exodus, which he describes as "against nature" (*contra natura*). He goes to the country that has freed itself from the protection and domination of his country, France. And also meets Muslims on their way to God. This is still very new at that time. The Second Vatican Council had just opened the doors of the church, recognizing that "the Catholic Church does not reject all that is true and holy in the great religions."[81] As a pioneer in this post-conciliar initiative, Christian then finds it difficult to enter the desired Algerian monastery—Notre Dame de l'Atlas—and to be understood by his superiors and brothers.

In addition to the difficulty of going to Algeria, Christian also found it difficult to enter the monastery he wanted in the place he wanted: in the Atlas Mountains. The community was fragile, the monastery very poor, and there were no monks who wanted to go there. There were major conflicts with the superiors, even one of them threatening to close the monastery. Only her unexpected death prevented this from happening.[82] In 1976, the monks decided to settle permanently in Algeria. The decision is

---

77. Salenson, *Christian de Chergé*, 43.

78. Christian spent many years discerning this vocation and elaborating a "theology of encounter."

79. Cf. Suzana Macedo's excellent work, "Louvor a uma só voz."

80. Ray, *Christian de Chergé*, 79.

81. *Nostra Aetate* n. 4; Ray, *Christian de Chergé*, 80–81.

82. Kiser, *Passion pour l'Algerie*, 309.

made after many hesitations and struggles, being a true "miracle of communion," as Christian himself says. He expressed to the community the desire to establish himself in Cistercian life in order to live his particular vocation there, listening to Islam. The monks unanimously accepted his profession. And four other monks came from France to vow for stability in Algeria. These, of a new generation, were already the fruits of the Second Vatican Council, a monastic presence among Muslims: exactly what led Christian to those mountains.[83]

What hurt the most for Christian, the mystic and prophet, was that his calling to monastic life is not to be understood as an authentic apostolic vocation. Even his friends told him that. The superiors wanted him to stay in France. The monastery he chose had an extremely precarious community and lack of resources. But he intimately felt a burning desire that grew day by day: to make a vow of stability in Algeria, exactly where the presence of order and monastery seems so precarious. Since 1952, no one has done this, but finally the Abbot of Aiguebelle accepts Christian's request. He pronounces his vows in this monastery, Notre Dame de l'Atlas, and he says: "This monastery is like the bride I chose, imperfect but unique."[84]

Pronouncing his final vows at the Feast of Saint Teresa of Lisieux, he said that the intimacy of the community is directly in line with his desire and the deep meaning of a consecration to the communion of saints. This is very present in his vocation and has a fundamental meaning in that it is a vocation for universal prayer, together with the saints of North Africa and "all the saints hidden in the Algerian, Pagan, Jewish, Christian or Muslim countries," to which he associates his parents, brothers, and sisters, the brother of prayer for one night[85] and his dear Mohammed.[86]

In August 1972, Christian explains to his community in writing the reason for his strong desire to enter that monastery in the midst of those mountains. In his words, Mohammed's act of love is very present. "In the blood shed by this brother who was murdered for not wanting to hate, I knew that my call to follow Jesus Christ would be to live the greatest love possible. I also knew that this consecration of mine must flow from prayer in order to give true witness to the presence of the Church."[87]

---

83. Ray, *Christian de Chergé*, 108.

84. Ray, *Christian de Chergé*, 82–84.

85. Chergé, *L'Invincible esperance*, 33–38.

86. Ray, *Christian de Chergé*, 109.

87. Kiser, *Passion pour l'Algerie*, 40.

Choosing to root his perpetual consecration in Algeria, Christian de Chergé is fully aware that he is now an invited guest of a people who welcome him. He longs for this dependence. In addition, he is changing the security and status of a respectable clerical career in France, where he could even be bishop, as his father wanted and hoped, for total insecurity and obscurity in Algeria. He is conscious and happy to be adopting a recently independent country, whose culture was dominated by the French. Now he would be that guest, totally dependent on the goodwill of his hosts. The member of the colonizing people humbly entered the colonized land, submitting to the culture of those once dominated by his people. This fills him with spiritual consolation. He understands himself and calls himself a "beggar of love."[88]

And according to his words, he finds everything he lacked in the rich parish of Sacré Coeur in Montmartre, Paris: a life of simplicity and poverty, "surrounded by a population that is poor but smiling, dignified and without bitterness. They are believers and respectful of all religious people, as long as they are consistent between what lies behind and what lies ahead."[89]

He is, however, equally aware of the perpetual insecurity and the great and kenotic dispossession that his calling imposes on him. Writing to a friend, he says: "The call I feel made me want to be a stranger who has no more home on this earth to go wherever God wants. But this same calling consecrated me to live a vow of stability in this monastery, to be a living incarnation with all the inhabitants of this country, this City of God where all the borders of country, race, and religion should one day disappear."[90] Because he felt this desire, he even applied to be nationalized as Algerian, a demand that cost him a good understanding with his father, who never accepted this gesture of his son and to which the Algerian government itself never responded.[91]

After his election as prior, he was, by grace of office, the rock and cornerstone of this group that has globally followed the prophetic intuitions of his presence in Islamic countries, even though it was not easy for the community as a whole to cope with his strong temper and his harsh and sometimes severe attitudes.[92] For example, Christian adopted a number of

<hr>

88. Kiser, *Passion pour l'Algerie*, 39.

89. Kiser, *Passion pour l'Algerie*, 39.

90. Kiser, *Passion pour l'Algerie*, 49.

91. Kiser, *Passion pour l'Algerie*, 49.

92. Henning, *Petite vie des moines de Tibhirine*, 20.

local habits to identify with Muslims, which were not as pleasant and easily assimilated by his brothers. During Ramadan, he fasted like his neighbors from dawn to sunset, maintaining their normal working hours, and saying, "The Eucharist is enough for me."[93] He also followed the tradition of taking off his sandals before entering the chapel as Muslims do.[94]

His privileged intelligence made him study and observe especially the mystics and the popular religion. He could then "draw lines from an age-wrinkled face, oppressed by successive make-ups, deformed by everyday reality." He thereafter writes and describes the marks of a spiritual current in Algeria, for which he wishes to be a link.[95] In this, he is encouraged by Cardinal Duval, who repeats unceasingly in his exhortations, that the Church is "ecstatic," meaning that it exists only in order to meet others—priests, religious, laity; they do not want anymore to convert their Muslim neighbors, but to live a brotherly friendship, as the council invited them to do, in order to recognize the presence of God and the action of the Holy Spirit in the Muslim faithful.[96]

But he also feels and suffers from the violence present in the country. How to make the monastery for which he was responsible a place of peace? Christian gives a spiritual answer to this question. He recalls a phrase from Paul Claudel in his message to the Germans: "A country is large when it makes the most of its spiritual resources when it treats human beings with respect."[97]

This concern was always present in him until the end. He absolutely wanted the monastery to be a place of peace. Three weeks before he was kidnapped, he preached a retreat during which he made the following recommendation: "'Thou shalt not kill': not to kill himself, not to kill time (which is God's), not to kill confidence, not to kill death itself (by trivializing it), not to kill the country, the other person, or the church. There are five pillars of peace: patience, poverty, presence, prayer, and forgiveness."[98]

The murder of a group of Croatian, Christian, and monastery-related people affects the whole community. And the fact that death must be given "in the name of Allah" brings Christian's suffering to paroxysm. Brother

93. Ray, *Christian de Chergé*, 105.

94. Kiser, *Passion pour l'Algerie*, 85.

95. Ray, *Christian de Chergé*, 98.

96. Ray, *Christian de Chergé*, 101.

97. Ray, *Christian de Chergé*, 56.

98. Olivera, *How Far to Follow*, 6.

Luke also comments: "Men never do evil as completely and joyfully as when they do it for religious reasons" (cf. Ps 43).[99] When the GIA (Groupe Islamique Armé) arrives on Christmas Eve, Christian talks peacefully and firmly with the group leader. This is a confirmation of his vocation to be a universal brother, whatever the cost.[100]

The community was frightened after this visit and expected the terrorists to return at any moment. The prior calls the group and listens to each and every one. They agree on three points: not giving money, getting together, and not endangering the neighbors who work with them. The idea of leaving with the first intimidation and leaving the people who trust them so much is not satisfactory to anyone.[101] The Christmas visit inaugurates a different mood in the community. In the free choice to stay, each one knows the risks. The community finds a "grace of natural cohesion." But not without much suffering.[102]

Community discernment to stay has the fruit of greater unity in the community. Christian writes to the general superior: "The facts that bring us infinitely closer do not erase the differences at all. . . . There is also an 'us' that moves, progresses in grace and wisdom."[103]

A very important fruit for the prior after the Christmas visit is to see that he can not only give but must learn to receive. He is living what he himself wrote about Charles de Foucauld in 1987: "The essence of the mission is to accept ourselves as dependent upon those to whom the Spirit has sent us, wholly surrendered in love, and in need of what they are, what they have the strength to give us from God." And he adds, "This was Brother Charles' second conversion to Tamanrasset at the time of his illness: to accept receiving."[104]

In this scenario of violence and insecurity, the Abbot General, Dom Bernardo Olivera, tells Christian that the Order needs monks and not martyrs. The Abbot General tells that the prior mystic made a deep silence, and then replied, "There is no contradiction." Dom Bernardo comments on this episode in a book written later: "Today I see that he was right: monks and martyrs. Order, the Church, the world, we all need faithful witnesses

99. Ray, *Christian de Chergé*, 178.

100. Ray, *Christian de Chergé*, 180.

101. Ray, *Christian de Chergé*, 182–83.

102. Ray, *Christian de Chergé*, 184.

103. Ray, *Christian de Chergé*, 188.

104. Ray, *Christian de Chergé*, 189–90.

who speak words of blood from the inexhaustible source of His first love. We need followers of Jesus who are ready to follow Him to the end, eager to embrace the cross of forgiveness that gives freedom and salvation. God gave us all this in the people of our brothers."[105]

Christian de Chergé's mysticism, which culminates in his testament—one of the most important spiritual texts of the twentieth century—is certainly the concrete demonstration that he was aware of his destiny and faced it in deep communion with his brothers and with his master Jesus Christ. But he included in this communion all his brothers and sisters of Islam who never left his heart.

Mysticism and Thinking of Christian de Chergé

The writings of this admirable Trappist, prior of the Tibhirine monastery, have only recently begun to be studied. And we have already found important studies that bring to light some treasures lived by this luminous figure that becomes ever-more important for present and future generations. Here we will try to reflect on some points about the mystic of Christian de Chergé, which are inseparable from his thinking.

Mysticism of Reconciliation of Differences

Christian is an assiduous reader of the French Jewish philosopher Emmanuel Levinas, who indelibly marks his reflection on the otherness and the difference of the other. Certainly the proximity to Levinas's philosophy contributed to the monk developing a mysticism and a reflection corresponding to this mysticism that are steeped in the otherness and vulnerability so present in the reflection of the Jewish Talmudist and philosopher.

The center of Levinas's philosophy is the epiphany that manifests itself in the face of the other, the different, the poor, and the oppressed, and which questions violence. Levinas defines the "other" in two perspectives: the metaphysical other and the other as a face.

> The Metaphysical Other is other of an otherness that is not formal, of an otherness that is not a mere identity inversion, nor of an otherness made of resistance to the Same, but of an otherness prior to every initiative, to every imperialism of the Same;

105. Olivera, *How Far to Follow*, 12.

another of an alterity that does not limit the Same, because in this case the Other would not be strictly Other: by the frontier community, it would still be within the system. The absolutely Other is Another; does not sum up with me. The collectivity in which I say "you" or "we" is not a plural of "me." I, you, are not individuals of a common concept.[106]

The way the Other presents itself, surpassing the idea of the Other in me, we actually call it the face. This way does not consist in figuring as a theme under my eyes, in exposing itself as a set of qualities that form an image. The Other's face destroys at every moment and surpasses the plastic image he leaves me, the idea to my measure and the measure of his ideatum—the proper idea. It is not manifested by these qualities, but kath'autó. It expresses itself.[107]

One can see—by reading the writings of the Tibhirine Trappist—how far Levinas's influence reaches Christian de Chergé's theology itself, impacting his conception of God and inspiring his prayer and action. And the Jewish Talmudist and philosopher even illuminates his reading of the Quran. For example, in his homily of December 10, 1995, he says:

Before the definitive establishment of the coming kingdom and where will we finally understand all the "Why"? of our differences (cf. Quran S. 5,48), this is the time of waiting for the Other. And it is primarily the time of MERCY. It is up to us to receive him with gratitude from the Totally Other, as obscure witnesses of a difference, the one Jesus introduces into the world, light in our darkness. The Spirit of wisdom and strength, counsel and discernment, knowledge and fear of the Lord presides over this difference toward which he directs all differences from "others" and my own, waiting for the Other: difference, my HOPE! Yes, truly, Lord, you are the Other we hope for![108]

Among the prior's writings there are many that testify to his passion for Islam and the Islamic religion and tell how he can find beauty in this difference between his faith and that of the other. Among these many texts, we first highlight one of them, considered to be especially significant. It describes a common prayer that Christian has with a Muslim in the monastery chapel. The description is very discreet and somehow mysterious. However,

---

106. Levinas, *Totalidade e infinito*, 26.

107. Levinas, *Totalidade e infinito*, 38.

108. Chergé, *L'Autre que nous attendons*.

it is most evident that the experience described therein is that of a common prayer made by two mystical men of different traditions.

There were three people that night in that chapel. Christian was one of them; the other was a Muslim that arrived later. And a third arrived later and did not quite understand what was happening there. The report makes it clear that this "third" who arrived eventually includes himself in the open and dialogical prayer.

Night of Fire[109]

Sunday, September 21, 1975, amidst Ramadan

A quarter of an hour after Completion, back to the chapel . . . Silence of the night, this beach on the shores of the Word, where all the words and noises of the day break like waves.

Gloom of the night, in the shadow of a Presence entrusted to the vigilance of the flickering lamp in the sanctuary.

Prayer of abandonment, prostrate, between the altar and the tabernacle: "Seek the Lord while he is found," said the Prophet Isaiah (today's liturgy).

And then, this other presence that comes close, sweetly, unusual.

You were there too, you too, very near the same altar, brother kneeling, prostrate.

The silence continues for a long moment.

A murmur rises from the depths, then amplifies itself, tearing itself into some abyss, as a peaceful yet irresistible source: 'AL- LAH! "God!" 'ALLAH" AKBAR! "The Big Whole!" I sigh. "God!" Again and again this sigh, like that of the nourishing child and not for a moment to catch his breath before asking again; the sigh of the one who knows to be insatiable prayer, and who is not satisfied with being there, turned so small toward the Totally Other.

Silence. Then you turned to me, "Pray for me." Another silence, your waiting. We had barely spoken a few words since your arrival Monday with him, our mutual friend. You remain there. I must risk words that I will hardly hear:

Only and Almighty Lord, Lord who sees us, You who unite everything under your eyes, Lord of tenderness and mercy, God who is ours, wholly.

---

109. The original is entitled "Nuit de feu," in Chergé, *L'Invincible espérance*, 33–38. The footnote to the title of the text reads: "This testimony was written by Christian a year after the meeting. It has no title. We think we can bring you closer to Blaise Pascal's celebrated experience, also titled 'Nuit de feu.' The translation is ours."

Teach us to pray together, You, the only Master of prayer, You who first attract those who turn to You, You, You, You . . .

From there our prayer became two voices. Arabic and French mingle, mysteriously come together, respond, merge and blend, complement each other and combine. The Muslim invokes the Christ. The Christian submits to God's plan for all believers, and one among them who was the prophet Muhammad.

Then both seek to penetrate together in the love that says God. They are both in the storm . . .

"Vacancies assault me, order peace!" You say

"Lord, save us, we perish!"

"Put your light in my heart, light my way," you say.

"Put a light in my eyes, a light in my lips, a light in my ears, a light in my heart. . . . I am the light of the world. You are the light of the world, which must not hide because it must shine to me. . . ."

The path narrows, while the denser silence still opens the common path toward the love of this shared God.

And it is you who launches. I welcome this.

"I do not ask you for wealth; I do not ask you for power or honors. . . . I only ask you for the Love that comes from You, for nothing is lovely outside of You and no one can love without You.

I want to love you in everything. Love is the source, the eye of religion. Love is the joyous consolation of faith."

The PRAISE then overflows the place and the moment. He takes us back in time to discover all the stages of God's long adventure in search of humanity, from Abraham, the Friend.

That's when he arrives, so does he. He was waiting for you, looking for you, surprised that he had not seen you come to the evening meeting for prayer before the second Ramadan meal he was taking with you. He has just entertained some guests at length, answering their questions about prayer "in the Spirit."

In the obscurity of the chapel, he did not notice but the murmur first. Intrigued, not daring to believe too much, he moved forward and we met us at work here together. Alas, he joined us. In fact, the Word came to us immediately: "Where two or three come together in My Name, I AM in their midst. What more to ask?

The prayer becomes wider, with more breath. A complicity to three, more demanding for the inner ear that one wants to be available in one's own way, strange, disconcerting at times; the impression of zigzagging in the sands! Let the prayer of one question the other in the deepest of silence without other voices, resume the flight, then jump toward the other charged with a new echo. Note after note, the symphony is built on the fusion of these three different expressions of one and the same faithfulness, that of the Spirit who is in God, who says God! Prayer against the temptations of Satan, "the stoned one"; then, together, the "fatihâ," the "Magnificat" (you repeat it word after word), the PATER (Our Father) (you know it by heart) and, always and yet, praise, thanksgiving.

Should it be said that we stopped? It was past 11 pm! Since 8 pm, we were there, side by side . . . all this time, an instant, is hard to believe!

Exuberant joy, each one on his side, each in his own way. Tomorrow, you will say you wanted to dance, then walked around the buildings four times, singing.

What if God himself laughs at the play he has just preached to centuries of cursing among brothers called to pray to Him?

And he, he really wanted to know how we had done that! You said to him, "When I saw him there, alone, I felt I had to co something. I was afraid, and then I was . . . there was such a force in me that pushed me . . ."

Before leaving us this Monday, we talked about something else.

It was a bit like it still burned us, so it couldn't be said without getting lost. "Fresh paint" must not be touched, otherwise it will stain completely.

You told me, "Everything is simple when God leads." That is all.

N.B.: Notes written on paper on September 24, 1975. Until this birthday (September 21, 1976) I have not seen this one-night brother. He exists. He tells me all the others.

This common prayer and its mystical moment lived in communion, each from their own tradition, very touchingly shows two men believing in God and the epiphany of the other. From this difference, the epiphany makes the humanly impossible happen: to pray to the God of the other, to rejoice in the faith of the other. It is also possible to experience a double ecstasy: to go from your own tradition to the other's tradition and to open oneself to be spiritually comforted by the other's experience and the other's tradition.

Mysticism of Forgiveness

Faced with the threat to him and his community, Christian has the opportunity to work within himself and help his community do the same toward forgiveness. Their situation brought the challenge of living the sermon on the mountain and the great and difficult calling of Jesus to their core: to forgive our enemies, to love those who mistreat us, not to return our offenses with similar offenses, and to build peace where violence is found.

From its beginnings, humanity has seen forgiveness as a difficult challenge to accomplish. And it had to go a long way through revenge, greater than the offense it received, followed by the limitation of violence with equivalent attitude and aggression.[110] The New Testament proposes a qualitative leap in this humane and humanizing attitude of forgiveness that makes human beings experience their transcendent potential in relation to other created beings.

The word "forgiveness" constitutively carries with it a whole anthropological and theological conception. It reveals that to be human is to exist and to move in an economy not of exchange, not of commerce, but of gift.[111]

We are made for the gift and not for the interested and commercial relationships that the consumer society imposes on us. Forgiveness represses and emphasizes that which is even constitutive of our identity. To forgive equals to persist in the gift; insist on giving. Even after the offense, do not let it rupture. It doesn't or won't happen because one party insists, persists, or forgives. In other words, accept the deficit, agree to have less.

The Judeo-Christian revelation and theology's reflection on it affirm that if we are like this, we do not exist alone. We are responsible for each other, we are connected to each other, and it is all up to us that humanity will continue to understand itself as made for the gift and not for the irresponsible accumulation of goods excluding others from them. It also reveals that humanity stops the irresponsible violence toward others and creation.[112]

And the biblical revelation says even more: we are like this because God is so like that. If we are created in his image and likeness, we cannot be otherwise. And if God is good and faithful and always forgives, persists in the gift, no matter what we do, for humanity to fulfill its calling as creature it can only forgive, insist, and persist in the gift of itself to God and others.

To acknowledge oneself imperfect, sinful, and in need of forgiveness will then amount to recognizing oneself called to forgive others. To persist in the gift so that others may find the full life for which they were created.

---

110. Cf. the so-called *lex talionis* (eye for an eye, tooth for a tooth). On this, see Bingemer, *Violência e religião*.

111. Cailler, *Une anthropologie du don*; Marion, *Etant donné*.

112. Cf. Pope Francis' recent encyclical *Laudato Si'*, which unites indissolubly the care of the earth and the care of human beings.

In the Jewish Bible, forgiveness is an important point not only of the relationship between God and humanity, but of the relationship between human beings among themselves. The feast of Yom Kippur is like the crowning of the process of awareness of the need to be forgiven and to properly forgive the elected people.

Bad deeds or transgressions have two polarities: one of man in relation to the other man, his fellowman; and the other, of the human being, male or female, in relation to God. The first is that of daily, outer, social, and interhuman life. The other, inner, happens in the secret of consciousness. The first is something human, and human beings have to resolve it: "Transgressions from man to man are not atoned for by Yom Kippur unless they are forgiven by others."[113] Hence, it is customary to ask for forgiveness; if they do not forgive, God will not intervene.

The religious feast of Yom Kippur is then intended to gather into the conscience of the pious Jew all the offenses committed by him during the year and of which he repents. The process of *teshuva* (repentance, return to goodness, conversion) cannot magically take place in one day. And in the month of Elui, the last of the year, the warning is placed for repentance and conversion in order to prepare to receive and give forgiveness and then celebrate the Kippur feast of atonement.

Atonement, Kippur, in the Hebrew root, refers to the "covering," that is, the punishment that involves the wicked act. The atonement does not erase the evil that was done. One can forgive, nullify, cease, or stop the punishment, but not the act committed; this act is there and the only way to overcome it is through a transcendental modification of later personal conduct in close coherence with the forgiveness given and received. The acts come from the sinful human being, and will remain his, and the consequence will remain his responsibility. God can erase the punishment, not the act. Fasting—which accompanies Yom Kippur all day long—does not work miracles nor have magical powers. It concentrates man again in his spirit by fasting and praying to be purified by forgiveness. After Yom Kippur, celebration and joy is expected, not losing sight of the fact that the holiday is a holy day of joy.

In Christianity, the conception of a God who always forgives is not only radicalized, he who is forgiveness and grace in himself, but also this conception is brought to higher levels, to the need to forgive each other always and at all times, no matter what magnitude of the offense suffered.

113. Peninei Halakha, "Sins for Which Yom Kippur."

The Sermon on the Mount, the great kingdom letter designed and proposed by Jesus of Nazareth, makes this very clear. In Matt 5:23–24 ("If you bring your gift to the altar, and there recall that your brother has anything against you, leave your gift there at the altar, go first and be reconciled with your brother, and then come and offer your gift"), for example, although situated in a cultural and ritual context, the teaching broadens and universalizes. Only the Christian united with his brethren through charity and capable of reestablishing the union where it was broken through his fault may turn to God, address his praises and requests, and beg his mercy. Matthew repeatedly insists on the forgiveness of the offenses endured as a condition of God's own forgiveness. (Matt 6:15: "But if you do not forgive others, neither will your Father forgive your transgressions." Matt 18:21–22: "'Lord, if my brother sins against me, how often must I forgive him? As many as seven times?' Jesus answered, 'I say to you, not seven times but seventy-seven times.'") It is understandable that he also underlines, strongly, what is required when dealing with the aggressor himself.

Forgiveness, therefore (Matt 5:25–26), is not an image, but a duty imposed on the Christian. The process itself is not fictitious, but it is a case that can take place within the communities (cf. 1 Cor 6:1: "How can any one of you with a case against another dare to bring it to the unjust for judgement instead of to the holy ones?"), and the character in question is, as before, the culprit who is obliged to apologize to his adversary.

What the evangelist means is that in the event that, for one's own fault, someone has a lawsuit with one of his fellow Christians, hurry to obtain his forgiveness, otherwise God himself will condemn him in the final judgment. God's forgiveness and human forgiveness are therefore inseparably linked when it comes to the economy of love that is threatened by sin and division.

Matt 5:38–42 states, "You have heard that it was said, 'An eye for an eye and a tooth for a tooth.' But I say to you, offer no resistance to one who is evil. When someone strikes you on your right cheek, turn the other one to him as well. If anyone wants to go to law with you over your tunic, hand him your cloak as well. Should anyone press you into service for one mile, go with him for two miles. Give to the one who asks of you, and do not turn your back on one who wants to borrow." By contrast, the evangelist expounds what is characteristic of Christians for him when he happens to be offended by his fellow men. However, the text causes some discomfort, because what follows the description of the violent aggression suffered points toward a conduct of total passivity with respect to mistreatment and aggression of all kinds. The evangelist wants to go further than Greeks and Jews who once knew how to ban revenge. What is original here is the extent the teaching takes, well beyond this particular aspect.

The general statement that opens the antithesis is already impressive: "But I say to you, offer no resistance to one who is evil" (Matt 5:39). These are human relations, where evil is therefore neither the devil nor evil in the abstract sense. These, indeed, are hostile powers to God, against which the New Testament commands and acts. But it is in man, in the wicked and violent human being that one must think here, the one whose evil nature produces acts harmful to others. Evangelical teaching here is aimed at all kinds of active wickedness, in which the Christian should neither participate nor resist in a similar manner, adopting an attitude of humble meekness before his persecutors.

"When someone strikes you on your right cheek, turn the other one to him as well" (Matt 5:39). Matthew is the only one to mention the "right face." This could be the fact that the right side is considered the most worthy in biblical literature, which apparently reinforces the extent of injury. Moreover, a slap received on the right cheek suggests that the blow was dealt with the reverse of the hand and is therefore more painful. According to the Jewish Mishnah, a blow with the reverse of the hand requires a double fine over a single slap. It seems indeed that the evangelist wanted, by this supplementary trait, to show how far the offended and beaten should go to have patience and a willingness to forgive.

"If anyone wants to go to law with you over your tunic, hand him your cloak as well" (Matt 5:40). It is not a matter of taking this teaching literally, but only this: instead of resisting the profiteer, grant to his claims more than he covets, and this in all detachment and gratuitousness. Donate more than is required and due.

The evangelist places after these two "invasions" of his own rights, the requirement to walk with someone one mile, which must be answered by walking two. Therefore, both the borrower and the one who lends must give all or more of what they ask and find joy in it. One must voluntarily lend oneself to the imposed service. What's more, go beyond the required measure. After acts that clearly violate justice, the evangelist places those who go beyond a royal right. It is up to the Christian *to go beyond that as well*, while still loving and being open to others who want to plunder him.

Following the passive attitude of earlier verses, the evangelist proposes to the Christian in Matt 5:43–47 an active code of conduct ("You have heard that it was said, 'You shall love your neighbor and hate your enemy.' But I say to you, love your enemies, and pray for those who persecute you, that you may be children of your heavenly Father, for he makes his sun rise on the bad and the good, and causes rain to fall on the just and the unjust. For if you love those who love you, what recompense will you have? Do not the tax collectors do the same? And if you greet your brothers only, what is unusual about that? Do not the pagans do the same?"). If he is asked to endure and bestow, he must still actively and dynamically love every man, including the one who harms him.

The principle set forth here implies passing beyond the love of neighbor which, according to the Law, retains a restrictive sense (loving as oneself), and the mention of the enemy expresses the antithesis suggested by the phrase that begins it: "Love your enemies." But what kind of love is it? It is not at all a spontaneous tenderness, made of affinity, which would indeed be impossible in such a case. The Greek term used to express what love is, the verb *agapan*, shows that this love derives from a will not compelled by the embarrassment that man must impose when it comes to enemies. Moreover, it is necessary to leave the purely psychological field, for charity must be exercised in the form of active goodness and come to concrete effects and benefits. It is, therefore, a love perpetrated by forgiveness. And that, therefore, not only repays, but restores.

The teaching, thanks to a technical word—"enemy"—is generalized, encompassing every situation where the Christian is mistreated, or even exposed to death because of his faith. As the following opposition (v. 46) confirms between the "brother" (the one who loves me) and the "enemy" (the one who hates and attacks me), this is neither the personal adversary within the religious community, nor the enemy of the nation in the political and military sense, but the persecutor of the faith, the enemy of the messianic community formed by the early Christians.

The repressed motivation of the evangelist to sustain such love and such demand is sought outside the world of creatures. The motive for sustaining such conduct is imitation of God himself, the desire to behave as a child of God. For Matthew, one becomes a child of God from the moment one begins to practice love for one's enemies, in imitation of that God who spreads his graces and benefits upon all men without distinction. Being a child of God is "proved" in faithfulness and obedience. And this conformity to divine will is already expressed in Jewish ethics in the form of imitation of divine conduct, in direct line with the conviction of being a man in God's image.

The Christian must go beyond the retributive justice of the scribes and Pharisees. Must do "more" than these categories, being limitless in forgiveness. God in person, by his sovereign example, calls him to a constant and limitless overcoming: "be perfect, *just as your heavenly Father is perfect*" (v. 48).

Jesus, the Son of God, drags his disciples to unsuspected limits. For he proposes not only an art of living in this world, but a positive obligation, a ministry of universal love. In this sense, it goes far beyond the very duty of forgiveness as conceived in Israel. Jesus' demand to love enemies goes so far as to reject what may still subsist of condescension in the forgiveness, to the point of forgetting so as not to think about anything but the generous gift of oneself, without any resentment and hidden intention. This enters into the full dynamics of the gift, in the world of restorative rather than retributive justice.[114]

It is simply a matter of love, without strategic peacekeeping moves on the frontiers of the church or propaganda for conversion. It is, therefore, and without doubt, a love more divine than human. But if the Gospel and, in it, the Sermon on the Mount, are proposed by Jesus Christ, they cannot, intrinsically and constitutively, be impracticable. In fact, what Jesus' pedagogy—a man of his time and culture—intended to show his disciples was that when it comes to giving and loving, what is done is never enough. That is why he urges them to forgive to the point of offering the other cheek, letting them strip off their clothes and yield to any demand.

114. Restorative justice emerges as a counterpoint to the traditional conception of criminal justice and punitive-retributive justice. The idea of creative restitution, the basis of restorative justice, was formulated by Albert Eglash and was consolidated in his article "Beyond Restitution: Creative Restitution," published in Joe Hudson and Burt Galaway's *Restitution in Criminal Justice*. This new vision of justice proposes a new paradigm in defining crime and the goals of justice. From this perspective, crime is conceived as a violation of the person and interpersonal relationships, and the role of justice should be to restore these violations, that is, to repair the damage caused not only to the victim, but also to society, the offender, and interpersonal relationships. On the contrary, punitive-retributive justice places crime as an act that merely violates state norm, and, in response to this conduct, imposes a penalty. In punitive-retributive justice, there is the centrality of state figures, punishment, and the attribution of guilt as a way to compensate for the consequences of the crime. See Zerh, *Trocando as lentes*, 174; and "Justiça restaurativa."

If the formulations of the Sermon on the Mount are rationalized, they run the risk of emptying them from their nectar, abandoning their assigned dynamic role: revealing the full breadth of the call to holiness, leading Christians to the radicality of meekness and forgiveness. Love, after all!

Recognizing this, Christianity, throughout its two thousand years of history, has also recognized that the Christian personally persecuted for hatred of the faith and who suffers death without opposing his executioner with armed resistance is thus eminently configured to Christ; it is martyrdom or baptism of blood, the quintessential testimony that has indelibly marked the beginnings of the church's life and is said to contain supernatural efficacy.

On the other hand, to those who do not receive this grace is the call to transfigure everything through the supernatural inspiration of all human activity and in particular the activity of transforming reality. So each of the Christian social behaviors—including the repression suffered—can, if lived in the dynamics of free gift, unbounding forgiveness, and love without borders, "complete" or "add," as St. Paul said, to the Christ's passion for his body, the church, in the service of redemption (Col 1:24).

Thus, in political action itself, a real love for the other—without excluding enemies—will be manifested in respect for people even through legitimate confrontations. Under these circumstances a Christian cannot be unjust, counterfeit, slanderous, capable of injuring, or killing in word or deed. A disciple of Jesus would expose himself/herself in defense of the truth, having as their only weapon the gospel of Jesus. These have been the actions of the prophets of our time: Martin Luther King, Monsignor Oscar Romero, Dorothy Day, and so many others, including Christian de Chergé.

When the murders of many religious people with whom the monks work occur, they feel that the possibility of a violent death is nearer. Christian reflects that "the community sign is the target, along with the differences it expresses."[115] However, he refuses to accept the title of martyr in the name of faith, thinking that this statement carries a form of integralism, the awareness of being "pure" in front of others who are not. "Jesus purifies, in effect, but through love. To the one who is not pure, he still says, 'Friend.' The only possible martyrdom is love. Jesus' testimony to death, his 'martyrdom,' is the martyrdom of love, of love for the human being, for all human beings. . . . And the martyrdom of love includes forgiveness."[116]

115. Chergé, *L'invincible esperance*, 197.
116. Chergé, *L'invincible esperance*, 193.

In Christian de Chergé's homily of July 17, 1994, he reflects on the recent death of two religious: a Marist brother (Henri) and a religious of the Assumption (Paul-Helene). And he notes that "this brutal death was inscribed in a continuity whose milestones became bright. Those who claimed his murder could not appropriate his death. She belonged to Other, like all the rest, since a long time." And he adds: "Maybe this is what we call 'Christians in remission.'"[117]

While the terrorist action speaks against Islam, the prior's love for this religion only grows, but not in an alienated mystical feeling that projects beyond the historical conflicts. He also assumes the facts, since his experience and conception of God is not of a God alien to human history. He accepts the risks of the present. Like his murdered religious companions, he is offered without defense. And that is to be in your place, the place God wants you to be in.

The great text about forgiveness that the prior of Tibhirine composes will surely be his testament, where he grants forgiveness to all, even to the one responsible for his death. Later, we will transcribe the whole of his text here.

<h2 style="text-align:center">Mysticism of Hope</h2>

The threat to the monastery is terrible. It is a situation where fear exists and is present. But it is constantly and daily overcome by hope. The dead religious are the obscure witnesses of hope, and Christian's mystical gaze upon them sees the resting for the future of the world.[118] Those who were killed did not wait for the persecutors to arrive to engage in the path of the martyrdom of hope, which, according to Christian, comes from the ancient monks in the desert and is what allows the Gospel to have something to say in today's world.[119]

In his homily of April 2–3, 1994, during the Easter Vigil, the prior speaks of the martyrdom of hope. Their characters are the women who come to Jesus' tomb full of fear, but with a hope they cannot name. They go to embalm him. And when they receive the glad announcement of the angel, they understand that the one they came to embalm is before them. The balm is without object. Hope is not embalmed on the march. It overtakes us, but

117. Chergé, *L'invincible esperance*, 193.

118. Chergé, *L'invincible esperance*, 193.

119. Chergé, *L'invincible esperance*, 193.

remains ahead, without us being able to circumscribe it.[120] The one we hope for cannot be seen. And only he can bring our hope to its right orbit, precisely because he precedes, in Galilee and to the ends of the earth.

He is no longer in this world and his witnesses feel that they are no longer of this world. Thus, Christian reinforces the hope of his listeners. We must be aware of this hope that has conquered death and the world. And in terms of a rare poetic beauty, the prior continues: "Behold, they are projected out of themselves into the unknown that crosses an empty tomb where the place has to be occupied. One must die to oneself, and without a word, for words are missing when the Word is no longer there to give them. . . . The women's muteness and fear lie at the exact juncture of the faith that knows how to speak, with fearlessness itself, and the hope that it must accept with its own logic made of silence and distance. The Holy Spirit will make the connection."[121]

Christian tries to convey to his community the sentiment he experienced at that time: they are all called to and destined for a martyrdom, that of hope. According to him, experienced in the Cistercian monastic life, "it is what always defines the monastic state: the step by step, the drop by the drop, the word by word, the body to body. . . . Here is the way in which 'he precedes us,' from beginning to beginning, by beginnings that have no end . . ." he says, quoting Gregory of Nyssa.[122]

Then lies this martyrdom and this hope: in their own Galilee, a monastic community wedged in the heart of Algeria in its Passover today. Only hope can keep them stable in their place. And they are helped by their neighbors, by the simple people who tell them the importance of their being there. "If you leave, your hope will fail us and we will lose ours."[123]

The homily rescues the elements that shape the hope of that expectant community from an obscure mystery that does not know exactly when and how it will be. "The insecurity of the place and the moment, the condition of foreigner, the reservation to be kept, is not the classic component of hope."[124] We must exorcise immediate fears and give them meaning and value in encounters with the Absolute of God. "Because,"

120. Chergé, *L'invincible esperance*, 426.

121. Chergé, *L'invincible esperance*, 426.

122. Chergé, *L'invincible esperance*, 426.

123. Chergé, *L'invincible esperance*, 426.

124. Chergé, *L'invincible esperance*, 426.

reminds the spiritual master Christian de Chergé, "even fears can help bring us closer to God."[125]

One must know that if everything goes on, nothing else will be as before. So it was for the women who were first witnesses of the resurrection. So also to all who knew how to wait against all hope. And from the bottom of the tomb of the one who precedes us on earth and in the sky that hope can spring "alive like a cry, the cry of the witness, the 'martyr,' from age to age: 'He is risen, Hallelujah!'"[126]

Mysticism of Charity

On Holy Thursday, March 31, 1994, Christian pronounced a homily on martyrdom, this time focusing on charity. In it he comments on something extremely controversial even today: the very conception of martyrdom, which in most traditional Christian theology is always linked to faith. The martyr dies and gives his testimony because of faith. It is out of hatred for the faith that he is persecuted, tried, condemned, and killed by the powers hostile to the faith.

As a man of his time, Christian de Chergé is fully aware that faith, in times of secularization and even postmodernity, does not exclude doubt or questioning. While the martyrs of faith were hard on their judges, understanding themselves as "pure" in the face of other "unclean" ones responsible for their death, with something of integralism, Jesus teaches that the only martyrdom is that of love, of charity. Even to the friend who betrays him, even to the one who is responsible for his death and to whom he has just washed the feet.

The martyrdom of Jesus is therefore martyrdom of love for the human being, for all human beings, even the outcasts, the thieves, the criminals, and those who act under cover of darkness and the dead of night. This martyrdom includes forgiveness, the perfect, endless gift that persists in giving. And Christian reminds his monastic and religious community that this is what they did by pronouncing their vows, giving their lives to God and letting them make use of them as they pleased.

It is still this love that guides them now, recalls the prior to his frightened, expectant community, his heart startling at the grave events he has been experiencing and the expectation unfolding before her. It is this love

125. Chergé, *L'invincible esperance*, 427.
126. Chergé, *L'invincible esperance*, 427.

that enables them to not take sides against each other or vice versa. In a theological, spiritual, and political choice, they chose not an impossible neutrality, but the infinite and universal freedom to love everyone, whoever they may be. And he remembers with very concrete words: "If I gave my life to the Algerians, I gave it to Emir S. A. He will not take it from me, even if he decides to inflict on me the same treatment he gave to our Croatian friends. And yet, I very much want him to respect it, in the name of the love that God has also inscribed in his vocation as a man. Jesus could not desire Judas' betrayal. Calling him 'Friend,' he addresses hidden love. He seeks his Father in this man. And I really believe he found him."[127]

He concludes by reminding his brothers that not only Christians bear this witness and live this martyrdom. In the history of the Algerian drama there are many authentic martyrs of simple and free love. So many, including Mohammed, to whom he owes his life. Where there is this love that gives one's life for another, there God will be, there will be martyrdom of charity.

It is this hope, this love, this innocence, this charity, this multiform and universal witness (martyrdom), which gives and will give strength to the testimony of the prior and of the whole community that lives in a state of epiclesis waiting for what will come. As Pascal says, "I don't believe in witnesses except those who are beheaded."[128]

A Community in the State of "Epiclesis"

Levinas's reading has a strong influence on the prior, especially when living the times of "epiclesis," according to his community brother Christophe Lebreton.[129] At this moment, in feeling that the siege of violence is narrowing, that violent death is a real possibility, and that the whole community is asked nothing more than to expect events that are likely to be painful and violent, it can be seen that Christian de Chergé's reflection and mysticism rescues elements of his readings and reflections from Emmanuel Levinas.

In one of the philosopher Talmudist's books,[130] he brings even the most radical consequences to his reflection on the other and its ethical

127. Chergé, *L'Autre que nous attendons*, 419–20.

128. Pascal, *Pensées diverses*, Lafuma 822; Brunschvicg 593; Tourneur 136.

129. Cf. extract from Christophe Lebreton quoted above.

130. Farias, "A anarquia imemorial do mundo," 18.34, especially 25, n. 13: The usual division of their texts—philosophical writings and confessional writings—meets an

"authority" over the self, its non-reduction to the extent of himself. It is the book *Autrement qu'étre ou au-dela de l'essence*[131] where the philosopher reflects on the importance of suffering for another, replacing oneself, bearing his pain. We can clearly see here the influence that Levinas's thought must have had on the mystic Christian de Chergé as he increasingly felt the thick and evident violence that tightened the siege around himself and his community. Also in his other works, Levinas develops the radicality of this responsibility for the other in his suffering and guilt to the point of taking it upon himself.[132]

Levinas declares that the self is always guilty,[133] even when nobody has done concrete harm. "Only I can, without cruelty, be designated as a victim. Exposing oneself to the burden imposed by the suffering and lack of others establishes oneself from self."[134] Thus, Levinas goes so far as to assert an astonishing radicality that the self is hostage to the other, and consequently the sole culprit and the only one to blame. "The hostage is the one to blame, for all his faults have fallen on him, and he can do nothing but offer to bear, suffer, give, and atone. The innocent and the justice that he carries come out of him to spread over others, of whom he is hostage."[135]

It is difficult not to associate the text of the homily given by Christian on Good Friday 1994, about the "martyrdom of innocence," where he comments on several recent events that cast the shadow of the cross and death on the monastery with this Levinasian reflection. Recalling the massacre

---

academic requirement that often hinders the reading of Talmudist Levinas—academic modesty—which ultimately impedes an interesting philosophical reception of so-called confessional studies. It is necessary to abandon the academic shame that, in the name of knowing no more than a kind of scientific rigor, often prunes the fluency of thought, its diversity of sources of inspiration. Levinas is far from a purist identity of thought. A consequent reading must recognize in his philosophy the voice of the Talmudist, and in his Talmudic studies, the voice of the philosopher. On the relationship between the Talmud and philosophy in Levinas's thought, see Chalier, "Levinas et le Talmud," in Chalier, *La trace de l'infini*, 235–52.

131. Levinas, *De Outro Modo*.

132. Levinas, *Entre nous*; Levinas, *Ethique et infini*.

133. Or "guilty." In French the same word designates both meanings: *coupable*.

134. Levinas, *Un Dieu homme?* 76.

135. Levinas, *Autrement qu'etre ou au-delà de l'essence*, 232 (our translation). Here we transcribe the original French: "L'otage est le seul coupable, car sur lui sont tombés toutes les fautes et il ne peut rien sauf s'offrir pour porter, souffrir, donner et expier. L'innocent et la justice qu'il porte sortent de lui pour se répandre sur les autres, desquels il est otage."

of several Croatian Christians, very close to the Tibhirine community, he recalls the words of his friend Gilles Nicholas: "This year the massacre of the innocent preceded Christmas!"[136] Filled with ardor and emotion, the prior expresses his feelings about the innocence of the victims:

> We confess at the same time the innocence of the child born on the night of Bethlehem and now found in the darkness of Golgotha. Let's not say, however, that our Croatian brothers were innocent little children. No more than us! This innocence that we equally recognize to them, we connect it directly to the torture they suffered: no, they had not deserved it! It would have taken a disproportionate, violently inhuman punishment to help us rediscover the track of innocence and proclaim it as founding every man's right to respect for his life. Rejecting the death penalty, even for criminals, not wanting the death of the guilty, and confessing this conviction.[137]

The background of Levinas's philosophy goes completely against this. For Levinas, the self does not express itself or become visible or self-understanding as self-conscious, but hypostatizes itself in another way: it is inextricably linked with a responsibility for others. The philosopher clarifies that this is not a slave alienation, although—and he uses here proper words of the process of human fertilization and gestation in the woman's body through the intervention of man—a "gestation" of the other happens in the same way as this responsibility: by the other means.

Levinas then proceeds, using a surprisingly sacrificial and expiatory speech that may intrigue the reader and has certainly received many readings and interpretations. This text is of particular interest to us in Christian de Chergé's interpretation, certainly given in a Christic and martyrdom situation:

> In exposure to wounds and outrages, in the sense of responsibility, the self is provoked as irreplaceable, as intended, without possible resignation to others and thus as incarnate to "offer oneself"—to suffer and to give—and thus, one and only suddenly in passivity, having nothing at all, that would allow him not to give in to provocation; one, reduced to himself and as contracted, as expelled in himself out of being.[138]

136. Chergé, *L'Autre que nous attendons*, 422.

137. Chergé, *L'Autre que nous attendons*, 422.

138. Levinas, *Autrement qu'être*, 134. Here we transcribe the original French for the sake of greater fidelity to the author's thinking, which may not be well conveyed by

Levinas considers that this constriction, that being "assaulted" by the weight of the other on one's own skin, is better than any metaphor for explaining the change that happens as a substitution of the other that implies the emptying—*kenosis* would say theology—of itself. This would be, according to Levinas, the last secret of the incarnation of the subject, prior to all reflection: an "indebtedness" "prior to any loan," an *a priori* deficit, as the echo of a sound that would precede the resonance of this sound. It is a passivity that is bottomless, absolute, and integral, provided that the persecuted person can be answered *by* the persecutor.

In pronouncing his homily, Christian is living in the horror of persecution, where so many have fallen and been innocent victims. He says, suffocated by the impression that all this gives him: "So much horror leaves you without a voice. We would almost blame ourselves for being still alive! What did they do to deserve this? What have we done more or less to still be there, intact?" Christian painfully experiences the wound of the shame of surviving the other's pain and death.[139]

He recalls what some say: that they, monks, being religious, are better protected, are safer, and are not like other foreigners. And he rejects this cheap consolation. "In us, solidarity speaks stronger than the simple right to life."[140] Christian refuses Pilate's dismissal of "innocence." He evokes the reaffirmation of Job's innocence: "Claiming not to be guilty with such stubbornness, do you not see, Job, that you are even more inhuman. . . . We have done nothing wrong and yet it is our fault!"[141] Christian reflects before his community gathered to celebrate the death of Jesus: "Who then is innocent? We are faced with the 'victim who has done nothing wrong' to accept his testimony, his martyrdom and to discover the unique and enveloping density of his martyrdom, that of innocence."[142]

It is the innocence of Jesus that Christian contemplates and invites others to contemplate. And he points out that in the face of this innocence

---

our free translation: "Dans l'exposition aux blessures et aux outrages, dans le sentir de la responsabilité, le soi-même est provoqué comme irremplaçable, comme voué, sans démission possible aux autres et, ainsi, comme incarné pour le « s'offrir »—pour souffrir et pour donner—et, ainsi, un et unique d'emblée dans la passivité, ne disposant de rien, qui lui permettrait de ne pas céder à la provocation ; un, réduit à soi et comme contracté, comme expulsé en soi hors l'être."

139. Chergé, *L'Autre que nous attendons*, 423.

140. Chergé, *L'Autre que nous attendons*, 423.

141. Chanteur, *Chronique d'une enfance meurtrie*.

142. Chanteur, *Chronique d'une enfance meurtrie*.

all symmetries fall to the ground. And it becomes impossible to remain only in claiming one's faults, as in an equitable division: these are my sins, those yours. Christian quotes the Quran, the book of Job, and the prophet Elijah. Only the Christ can claim to have never committed sin. And yet he never claimed to be "innocent." Nor did he wash his hands. Neither did he accuse others, because innocence does not accuse. On the contrary, God made him sin, as Paul says mysteriously.[143]

In this moment of persecution, fear, and violence that begins more clearly and will last for two years even before the community's abduction and subsequent martyrdom, Levinas's philosophy will certainly have closely followed the prior who should not only live but lead the discernment of the community toward their decision that will make it defenseless, faithful, and stable, alongside all the victims, in a time of innocent and patient waiting. Everyone should learn that innocence does not accuse, but assumes, takes over, suffers, and expiates.

As Levinas says:

> The face of his neighbor in his persecuting hatred may, by its very cruelty, obsess with a pitiful misconception or riddle that, without theft, only the persecuted deprived of all reference (as deprived of all resources and all help—and therein lies your uniqueness or your unique identity!)—can bear it. Submitting to the other is not absolute patience unless this "to the other" is already "for the other." This transference . . . and subjectivity itself . . . in the suffering endured to ask for this suffering . . . is not to extract from the suffering any magical virtue of rescue, but in the trauma of persecution to pass from the outrage borne to the responsibility of the persecutor and, in this sense, from suffering to atonement for the other.[144]

143. 2 Cor 5:21.

144. Levinas, *Autrement qu'être*, 141. See the original French: "Le visage du prochain dans sa haine persécutrice peut, de par cette méchanceté même, obséder pitoyable— équivoque ou énigme que sans se dérober, seul le persécuté privé de toute référence (en tant que privé de tout recours et de tout secours—et c'est là son unicité ou son identité d'unique !) est à même de supporter. Subir par autrui, n'est patience absolue que si ce « par autrui » est déjà « pour autrui ». Ce transfert—autre qu'intéressé, « autrement qu'essence »—est la subjectivité même. « Tendre la joue à celui qui frappe et être rassasié de honte », dans la souffrance subie demander cette souffrance (sans faire intervenir l'acte que serait l'exposition de l'autre joue), ce n'est pas tirer de la souffrance une vertu magique quelconque de rachat, mais dans le traumatisme de la persécution passer de l'outrage subi à la responsabilité pour le persécuteur et, dans ce sens, de la souffrance à l'expiation pour autrui. La persécution ne vient pas s'ajouter à la subjectivité du sujet et à sa vulnérabilité ; elle est le mouvement même de la récurrence."

Apart from the Lithuanian/French Jewish philosopher, another influence—this time from a woman—is felt on the prior. Christian medi-
tates and shares with his community the diary of a young Jewish mystic,
Etty Hillesum, and one phrase catches the eye: "If peace is established,
one day, it will not be able to be authentic unless each individual makes
peace within himself, exterminates every feeling of hatred for any race or
anyone. Whatever it is, or control that hatred and turn it into something
else, maybe even in the long run, in love—or is it too much to ask? And
yet it's the only solution."[145]

Accompanied by these two Jewish masters who inspired his spirituality, Christian de Chergé can be to the end at the head of his community
and walk along with it to the destiny that turned out to be his own. His will,
written long before the kidnapping of his victim, gives clear evidence of
how he prepared spiritually for whatever might happen.

A Testament to the Twenty-First Century

Christian de Chergé's testament—one of the most important spiritual
texts of the twentieth century—is certainly a concrete demonstration that
he was aware of his destiny and faced it in deep communion with his
brothers and his master Jesus Christ, but without failing to include in this
communion all his brothers and sisters of Islam, who never failed to have
a special place in his heart. The end of his life was lived with a universal
openness to all, thus imitating God himself, a mystery of universal self-
communication, ever and forever.

The prior composed this testament over a month: from December
1, 1993, to January 1, 1994.[146] Gerard de Chergé, younger brother of the
prior of Notre Dame de l'Atlas and his godson, was the depository of
this precious text. On May 23, 1996, he received the news that shook
France and the whole world: the seven monks of the Tibhirine monastery,
kidnapped two months earlier, on March 23 of the same year, had been
slaughtered. Gerard pulled a sealed envelope from his desk drawer that

---

145. Hillesum, *Diarios*.

146. Chenu, organizer of the Christian textbook *L'invincible esperance*, who we have
already quoted here, says in a note on p. 221 that December 1—the date he began writing
the will—is also the date of the murder of Father Charles de Foucauld in 1916. Chenu
notes that Christian was certainly sensitive to this date.

his brother Christian had sent him on February 13, 1994, from Fez, Morocco. It was inserted in a letter that began with the following words: "My only and favorite godson . . ."

In the letter, Christian asked Gerard to keep that envelope and not open it unless his death was announced. Very moved, Gerard went to his mother Monique de Chergé's house with the envelope. It was there, at his mother's lap, "his first Church," his mother in the flesh and faith took note of the message that the prior of Tibhirine addressed not only to his family, but to his community, the church, the Algerians, and more broadly, to men of goodwill. A few days later, the seven brothers and sisters gathered around their mother and decided that this text was not intended exclusively for them. They sent it to the newspaper *La Croix*, which published it on May 29.

From there the prior's will and spiritual testament to that small, dark monastery in the Atlas Mountains was reproduced in newspapers around the world, inspiring religious people and intellectuals, and becoming the subject of commentary and interpretation, inspiring the prayer of many people, and most recently appearing in the film by Xavier Beauvois, *Des hommes et des dieux*, in 2011.[147]

In it is poured the whole soul of the prior: his faith, his hope, and his love; his passion for Islam and the Muslims; his surrender without reservation and without turning back on God and the Algerian people; and also his deep desire to forgive his enemies, even the last-minute "friend" who wouldn't know what he was doing; and, above all, his conviction that God is universal love, who does not take sides with some more than others, does not save some to the detriment of others, and does not populate his paradise with only the "pure" or those belonging to a certain ecclesiastical or religious institution.

As a Christic figure, Christian de Chergé deeply marked his community. The strength of his faith and the stature of his spirituality were certainly decisive elements for this small, fragile, and vulnerable community to live all the stages of this long martyrial process that ended with their deaths as witnesses.

147. In the US entitled *Of Gods and Men*.

Facing a GOD-bye . . .
Spiritual Testament of Christian de Chergé:[148]

If it happened to me someday—and could be today—to be a victim of the terrorism that now seems to want to encompass all foreigners living in Algeria, I would like my community, my Church, my family, to remember that my life was GIVEN to God and to this country.

May they accept that the One Master of all life could not be indifferent to this brutal departure. Let them pray for me: How would I be worthy of such an offering? Let them know how to associate this death with so many other violent ones, left in the indifference of anonymity.

My life is worth no more than another life. It has no less value either. In any case it does not have the innocence of childhood. I have lived long enough to know myself complicit in the evil that seems, unfortunately, to prevail in the world, and even in the one that would blindly strike me.

I wish, when the time came, to have a moment of spiritual clarity that would allow me to ask for God's forgiveness and that of my brothers in humanity, at the same time, to forgive wholeheartedly those who would have struck me.

I could not wish this kind of death; It seems important to me to profess it. I do not really see how I could rejoice in the fact that these people I love are indiscriminately accused of my death.

It is very expensive to pay what will perhaps be called the "grace of martyrdom" by attributing it to an Algerian, whoever he is, especially if he claims to act in fidelity to what he believes to be Islam.

I know the contempt with which we could surround the Algerians taken globally. I also know the caricatures of Islam that a certain Islam encourages. It is very easy to have a clear conscience, identifying this religious path with the extremism of its extremists.

Algeria and Islam, for me, are something else, they are body and soul. I have proclaimed it a great deal, I openly believe what I have received from it, so often finding this guiding thread of the

148. Chergé, *L'Invincible espérance*, 221–24. Inch'Allah means "God willing." And the title (in French: *Quand un A-Dieu s'envisage*) includes two very expensive elements to the prior: 1. The expression "A-Dieu," used by Jacques Derrida to bid farewell to his recently deceased master Emmanuel Levinas; 2) the expression "s'envisager," which means to be on the horizon, to be considered, is composed of the word "visage," which means face in French, also used by Levinas, in which Christian certainly often meditated upon contemplating the face of his Muslim brothers.

Gospel learned from the knees of my mother, my first Church, precisely in Algeria, and already, with respect for the faithful Muslims.

My death, of course, will seem to give reason to those who quickly treated me as naive, or idealistic: "Let him say now what he thinks of this!" But those here must know that my most searing curiosity will be finally released.

Behold, I may, if it please God, dip my gaze into that of the Father to behold with him his children of Islam as he sees them, enlightened with the glory of Christ, fruits of his Passion, invested with the gift of the Spirit whose secret joy will be always to establish communion and re-establish resemblance, playing with differences.

This lost life, totally mine, and totally yours, I thank God that seems to have wanted it all for this JOY—there, against and in spite of everything.

In this THANK YOU where everything is now said of my life, I surely include you, friends of yesterday and today, and you, oh friends here, beside my mother and father, my sisters and my brothers and your own, tenfold as promised!

And you, the last minute friend, who wouldn't have known what you were doing. Yes, to you too I give this THANK YOU, and this "GOD-bye" in whose face I contemplate yours.

And may we be allowed to meet again, happy thieves, in paradise, to please God, our Father, mine and yours. AMEN!

Insha Allah!

The Free Choice of a Prayer Community

The decision made by the Atlas brothers—to stay where they were and not to leave as they could—is neither unique nor isolated. The then general abbot Bernardo Olivera explains:

> All those belonging to the Benedictine-Cistercian tradition have made a vow of stability. This binds us to death to a community and a place where the community lives. Many communities of our order have faced war and armed violence over the past few years and have had to seriously reflect on the significance of this vote and make the crucial decision to stay where they are or to leave.[149]

149. Olivera, *How Far to Follow*, 16.

The abbot general continues:

> During the twentieth century two other communities of our or-
> der gave us true martyrs of a living faith for the church and the
> world. The seven brothers of Notre Dame de l'Atlas simply offered
> us the same testimony of love and faith. In each of the three cases
> we are dealing with the grace given to the community, not just to
> an individual person. In a cenobitic context such as the Cister-
> cian monastery, the fact of life lived and given in community is
> particularly significant. This communal grace of martyrdom will
> also be grace to and from the church. We can already see the love
> of our brothers for the Church of Algeria and its local church in
> Algiers.[150]

His life and death are inscribed in the register of all those religious people, Christians or Muslims, who lived and gave their lives for God and others.[151]

In the discernment that led to the decision to remain in the Atlas Mountains, despite the tense situation surrounding them, the monks were aware of the possibility of a violent death. The letter that Father Christian de Chergé wrote to the abbot general after the murder of two religious in September 1995 said this clearly:

> The memorial celebration had a beautiful atmosphere of serenity
> and self-giving. He assembled a very small church whose remain-
> ing members were fully aware that from now on their presence
> must logically include the possibility of a violent death. To many,
> this is like a new, radical immersion in the charism of their con-
> gregation . . . and a return to the source of their first calling. At the
> same time, it is clear that all of us want none of these Algerians,
> to whom our consecration binds us in the name of God's love for
> them, to hurt this love by killing any of us or any of our brothers.[152]

Violence and threats will add nothing to the monastic vocation of the Notre Dame de l'Atlas community. They will only show to what extent their life was already given, *a priori*. The monk vows go for stability and this leads them to a community, but also to a country, to a people. The life of the monks was marked by the love of the people for whom they were guests. This love has been proved intensely. If tension had grown since 1992, it was

---

150. Olivera, *How Far to Follow*, 21.

151. Olivera, *How Far to Follow*, 21.

152. Olivera, *How Far to Follow*, 21, 19.

toward the end of 1993 that the danger really approached the monastery.[153] And the community had to live it to the end. It is in fire that gold is tested and the life of the monks has gone through this trial of fire.

The presence of death is not new to the monk and monastic spirituality. On the contrary: traditionally it is a faithful and constant companion. This is what Christian's brothers wrote in a circular letter from 1995. "This companion (the death) took a more concrete acuity with the direct threats, the upcoming murders, certain visits. . . . They were offered to us as a test, of veracity, useful, and not very comfortable."[154]

Experiencing this closeness, the community felt more free than ever. When the GIA came on Christmas Eve, the group chief said to the prior, "You have no choice." "Yes, we have a choice," replied the prior, expressing the *a priori* gift of his life and his unfailing attachment to the freedom of each one. The monks, following Father Christian's suggestions, meditated on the writings of Etty Hillesum, who touched them with indescribable force, especially this passage: "You know that I have the power to make you die," says the executioner. And the martyr has this answer: "you know that I have the power to be killed."[155]

What his communal martyrdom shows—and this is why he marks and seals the spirits so deeply and durably—is that deep down in silence and invisibility the fire remains. And it's not erased by the ocean of lukewarm and intimate stunts where we live.[156]

153. Henning, *Petite vie des moines de Tibhirine*, 39.

154. Letter of November 11, 1995; Henning, *Petite vie des moines de Tibhirine*, 51.

155. Henning, *Petite vie des moines de Tibhirine*, 44.

156. Frappat, *La Croix*, 1996.

CHAPTER III

The UCA as an Intellectual, Apostolic, and Community Project

Educated Jesuits, not by eagerness to be learned and to accumulate titles for show, but to be able to know more and better the Lord and his brethren the men, to take the Good News to the Church and the world we are sent to. For this we need to contemplate, with intelligent love, humanity and the ways of God with it. From this wise knowledge our own Cardoner should emerge, that is, the personal and broad view of the divine-human reality that allows us to aim and work from the perspective of contemplation to achieve love. The more educated we are, the more we will know how to get rid of the crust with which time and every culture covers the evangelical message, to return to its original freshness. Educated we will know how to translate and inculturate the message of Jesus according to places and people. We will understand better the missions that the Church entrusts us, understanding more profoundly its intention, being able to practice an intelligent and creative obedience. Instructed that we can continually go unmasking the ideologies that as humans always pinch us and that give us a true and up-to-date view of reality. Instructed to understand a better world ever more complex and diverse in culture and religiosity, as well as in the technological, communicational, social and economic fields. Instructed to be efficient instruments to the service of the Church.

—John Ochagavia SJ, "Instruidos y pobres," in *Revista Mensaje* 55.554 (November 2006)

IGNATIUS OF LOYOLA WAS not a man of letters when he experienced the divine presence and discernment of the spirits that transformed him from a military nobleman to a pilgrim of God's will.[1] Yet he always felt within

---

1. Ignatius, *Autobiography*.

him that intelligence—one of the seven gifts of the Holy Spirit[2]—which is a key point in God's human creation.[3] He also felt that developing intelligence effectively makes the human being more human and thus able to give greater glory to God. This is also the reason why he was, at the age of forty, studying at the University of Paris, always with the aim of serving God better. There he found his first companions.

When Ignatius founded the Society of Jesus in the mid-sixteenth century, he was very aware that its members should be poor and educated, that is, instructed.[4] Instructing themselves would imply conveying what they knew, that is, teaching others. This should be one of the occupations in which those formed by his spiritual exercises should work.[5] The intellectual apostolate, therefore, was present in the Society of Jesus from the beginning. So too, and closely linked to the first, was the educational apostolate, since one of the first fields where the Jesuits exercised their apostolate was education.[6]

From the earliest days of the Society of Jesus in Rome and during Ignatius' life, the nascent order was concerned with education. Later, and for centuries, the Jesuits developed academic excellence in the service of humanity. However, from the beginning, education was conceived by Ignatius as not only a theoretical occupation, but also and above all an instrument of formation.[7] People who have passed through Jesuit schools

2. The seven gifts of the Holy Spirit are: wisdom, intelligence (understanding), counsel, knowledge, fortitude, piety, and fear of God.

3. Cf. for example, at the very beginning of his pilgrimage in search of God's will, the illumination he had by the Cardoner River, where he says, "And while he was sitting there, the eyes of understanding began to open; and not seeing any vision, but understanding and knowing many things, both spiritual things, things of faith and letters. And this with such a large illustration that all things seemed new to him. And it is not possible to declare the particulars that then understood, although they were many, but it received a great clarity in the understanding, such that in all the course of its life, until the sixty-two years, collecting all the aids received from God, and all the things he knew, though he put them all together, did not seem to have achieved him as much as he did that once" (Ignatius, *Autobiography*, n. 30, our translation).

4. Right from the beginning, what Ignatius wants from the Jesuits is for them to be companions of Jesus as "poor and learned," in Casas, "Los jesuitas y la Universidad," 9.

5. O'Malley, *First Jesuits*, 212–13.

6. Cf. O'Malley, *First Jesuits*, 212–13. John O'Malley argues that the fundamental motivation that leads Jesuits to take up education as an important and even fundamental apostolate would be the opportunity to work with the same public for a long time and to convey to them the values by which the same order was moved.

7. Ochagavia, "Instruidos y pobres," 1.

and colleges have always been called not only to learn and teach, but—after receiving this training—in turn to form others in order to transform reality and make it more in the heart and soul to God's desire.

The Jesuit educational tradition consisted essentially of three parts: 1) a literary tradition based on the poetry and prose of ancient Greece and Rome (the "colleges"); 2) a philosophical and theological tradition based on Greek ethics, natural philosophy, and metaphysics (the Jesuit universities); and 3) these two traditions were enriched and perfected by the Western Christian tradition, in which "spiritual conquest" through the conversion of the "other" was an essential component.[8]

These three traditions that constituted the Jesuit tradition are radically Western, and from that gave the action of the new order a similar configuration befitting the culture of the West. It is necessary to be aware of the history of this tradition, not for the sake of merely historical interest *per se* but for the need to know the method that governed this institution, the way in which aspects of that history are used to benefit the present. Moreover, these "aspects" are, in most cases, the most profound and therefore the most culturally transcendent of the mentioned tradition.

This is the foundation of the Jesuit tradition of education. This is also the reason why the Jesuits decided in the early days of the founding of the order to assume formal education as a ministry; more so, as its main ministry. The basic premise of the tradition was that a training in "good literature" produced reflective individuals, inspired them to noble behavior, and was beneficial to society in the broadest sense through the honest, polite, articulate people who would emerge from the educational institutions set up by them. This formation is dedicated to promoting the common good.[9]

In the fifteenth century, universities were concerned with only two things: 1) intellectually solving problems; and 2) achieving professional success through the acquisition of professional skills. These remain the same top concerns as today's universities. Higher education institutions in general, from a humanistic point of view, have never seen the growth of the common and public good as priorities. Rather, they focused their efforts on training individuals who could later be successful practitioners or "cutting-edge" intellectuals. In contrast, the humanistic style of education applied by the Jesuits was radically centered on students as human

8. O'Malley, *First Jesuits*, 212–13; O'Malley, "How Humanistic."

9. O'Malley, *First Jesuits*, 212–13.

beings, and also concerned with making them responsible and committed to the common and public good.

A well-formed human being would be a good leader in society and could then develop a healthy nation. This was the basic logic that could be perceived behind the humanistic program the Jesuits created and adopted. It was the person-centered priority of the humanistic philosophy of education that prompted the priests and brothers of the Society of Jesus because it coincided with its equally person-centered religious program.[10] Nothing is more centered on the person and his freedom than the *Spiritual Exercises of St. Ignatius*. They were, therefore, the matrix for the entire apostolate of the Society of Jesus, including the educational apostolate. Once the program was adopted, they also saw it as capable of promoting the common good, even a specifically secular and civic good.[11] With their ministry of formal education, the Jesuits were then committed to a civic mission that was well rooted in reality.

Jesuit education, therefore, from the beginning tried to unite charity and intelligence. Intelligence in the service of truth and charity, and therefore of the greater good. There are five focal points of John O'Malley's reflection that help emphasize aspects of this tradition that are useful to today's world:[12]

1. Humanistic education, which helps students get out of the hidden confines of their present-day experience, gets them to ask questions, not just about their area or profession, but about life itself. On a more personal level, the study of "literature" reveals us to ourselves.

2. "Cultural perspective" is the study of the past to understand the present, and at the same time to have a point of comparison with other cultures.

3. Openness to others: "We are not born just for ourselves."

4. "Perfect eloquence." The study of literature provides a good command of language. As Socrates said 2,500 years ago, "Proper use of language is the surest sign of understanding."

5. The esprit de finesse. Adapt and accommodate. Make wise decisions.

10. O'Malley, "How Humanistic."
11. O'Malley, *First Jesuits*, 212–13.
12. O'Malley, *To Travel.*

It is important to say that for the Jesuits, an educational institution aims at evangelization and acts as a means of education. Evangelization, then, is what made the Society of Jesus a global institution because the Christian mandate consists essentially of "going to make disciples of all nations."[13] The goal is to teach the Gospel to everyone, to every creature. It was this mandate and its reception by the apostolic college that inspired Ignatius and his companions in founding the Society of Jesus. They founded an order that was by profession and first of all a missionary institution founded for the propagation of the faith.[14]

The Jesuits promised God "to travel to any part of the world where there is hope of greater service to God and the good of souls," whether "among the Turks, or in the New World, or with the Lutherans, or for any others, to be faithful, or infidels."[15] The dark side of evangelization and the cultural imperialism that characterized them so deeply is, in the opinion of many, intrinsic to them. Valignano, Ricci, and others have had to struggle with this problem in the past, and today it is still one of the most burning theological issues when thinking about the apostolate of the Society of Jesus.[16]

The Society of Jesus was and is today a global institution, spread across the four corners of the world and present on five continents of the globe. And this fact has shaped the tradition of their education in different ways. For example, the order can no longer recruit most of its members in Europe. Moreover, if the trends of Jesuit vocations continue as they have been so far with regard to this recruitment of the members of the Society of Jesus, within thirty years 75 percent of their contingent will be from Asia and Africa. This

13. Matt 28:19–20.

14. The founding label of the Society of Jesus, approved by Pope Paul III in 1540, contains the principles of the Institute's Formula. Its first lines pray that the "Society of Jesus was founded to fight in particular for the propagation and defense of the faith and the improvement of souls in Christian life and doctrine."

15. Cf. the Institute's Formula. The pontiff approved orally on September 3, 1539, the Formula of the Instituto da Companhia de Jesus, to which the confirmation was followed on September 27, 1540. The Formula, in the second essay approved by Pope Julius III in 1550 states as objectives of the order "the defense and propagation of faith and the perfecting of souls in Christian life and doctrine." The availability expressed by the founding group before the Supreme Pontiff was consecrated by the introduction of a special vow of obedience to the pope. By this fourth ballot, which add to the vows of chastity, poverty, and obedience proper to the religious, the professing Jesuits undertake to accept the missions that the Pope entrusts to them, in any part of the world.

16. For this issue of Jesuit cultural imperialism, see Deslandres, "Examplo aeque ut verbo" 258–73, especially 267. See also on this issue, with very original and profound treatment, the recent film *Silence* by Martin Scorsese.

will certainly have an impact on all the apostolates of the Society of Jesus and especially the educational ones we are studying here.

But even with all these changes, the broad horizon that Ignatius gave his Jesuits through the experience of the *Spiritual Exercises* and the landmark constitutions of the Society of Jesus marked the Jesuit vocation with a great freedom to find different ways to evangelize. And education was one of the most important. This is why schools and universities have been present since the beginning of the Jesuit life—trying to firmly combine intelligence, charity, and service. Jesuit universities must therefore be understood within this framework, at the same time charismatic and institutional.

What Is a Confessional University?

The classic description of the role of the confessional university comes from John Henry Newman, who elaborated on it around the mid-nineteenth century in Catholic Ireland. Three contributions are considered important within Newman's conception of the "idea" of a university:

1. Students learning to think clearly and accurately;

2. The university as an intellectual community;

3. The autonomy of each field of knowledge and the value of knowing as an end in itself.[17]

The commentators of the great John Henry Newman condense in these three points the synthesis of what is most important in his contribution to the idea of university.[18] This is of seminal importance, mainly because of the importance given to knowledge as a value in itself.[19] In contrast to Newman, less emphasis can be seen at a university such as El Salvador's Jesuit UCA—an institution that is our object of study here—over knowledge as an end in itself and more in its utility to transform the unjust reality of the country where it is located.[20]

The university in the model proposed by Newman aimed more at the faith of the people who would attend the university. Moreover, despite being English, Newman spoke to an Irish audience, which had been

17. Newman, "Idea of a University."
18. Ker, *Achievement of John Henry Newman*; Pelikan, *Idea of the University*.
19. Beirne, *Jesuit Education*, 44.
20. Beirne, *Jesuit Education*, 36.

oppressed for centuries, culturally, linguistically, and territorially by England's colonizing Protestantism. Newman saw the university as a bulwark for their faith and a means of gaining respectability, credibility, and even equality in civil society.

But the university model he presented left that society largely untouched. Social change was just beginning to be mentioned in Catholic circles. On the other hand, and positively, the university allowed Catholics no longer to be deprived of a university education. This is why he values knowledge so much in itself, thus responding to those who classified liberal education as useless and theology as unintellectual. Newman University has tried to deal with this kind of reality. And it retains relevance, although it also has limitations.[21]

In the thinking and discourse of the more contemporary Catholic Church, the confessional university is conceived as "a center of creativity and dissemination of knowledge for the good of humanity."[22] And it must be distinguished by the free pursuit of the totality of truth about nature, man, and God, "just as it must" search every aspect of truth in its essential connection with the ultimate truth, which is God.[23] The document that reflects on the confessional university is the Apostolic Constitution "Ex Corde Ecclesiae" by John Paul II.

For the Polish Pope, the confessional university—Catholic—has four essential characteristics:

1. A Christian inspiration not only for individuals, but for the university community as a whole;

2. A continued reflection in light of the Catholic faith about the growing treasure of human knowledge, for which it seeks to contribute with its own research;

3. Fidelity to the Christian message as it comes through the church;

4. An institutional commitment to the service of the people of God and the human family on their pilgrimage to the transcendent goal that gives meaning to life.[24]

---

21. Newman, "Idea of the University."

22. John Paul II, Apostolic Constitution "Ex Corde Ecclesiae," n. 265.

23. John Paul II, Apostolic Constitution "Ex Corde Ecclesiae," n. 267–68.

24. John Paul II, Apostolic Constitution "Ex Corde Ecclesiae," n. 269.

The last part of the papal document dictates general norms and insists that a professor of Catholic theology must have the *"missio canonica,"* that is, a mandate to teach theology in that institution. Some episcopal conferences from different countries or universities governed by religious orders and that are not pontifical have made their own statutes and bylaws that take into account the role guidelines, but which add their own elements to the profile of the institution they manage. Many Jesuit universities fit this model.[25]

The UCA in El Salvador has a unique status. Technically speaking, it is not a Catholic university, but rather understands itself as a university of "Christian inspiration," agreeing with many of the values set forth in "Ex Corde Ecclesiae." But it does not respond directly to the local bishop, invoking total freedom for its academic reflection and institutional action. While Monsignor Romero was archbishop of San Salvador, there were never greater doctrinal about what was taught at the UCA, nor events that could be negative to the university's profile.[26] For this reason, the UCA could affirm its model while Ignacio Ellacuría was dean, from 1979 until 1989, when the assassination of Ellacuría along with his community occurred. The university was in tune with the movement taking place in Latin America at that time.

The Inspiration of the Historical-Ecclesial Moment of the Continent

In the twentieth century, after the Second Vatican Council, a new movement began in Latin America. This new movement received the news brought by the council and sought to reread it from the Latin American reality of poverty, injustice, and oppression. This "reception" inextricably linked evangelization with the struggle for justice and gave rise to a conception of evangelization and pastoralism that did not undergo the transformation of reality. This obviously meant having a critical stance on the spread of the Gospel, as it had been for four centuries, since the dawn of Iberian colonization on the continent. Such evangelization, and

25. See for example, the various Jesuit universities in the United States and even some in Latin America that do not have the local bishop as grand chancellor and therefore have professors who enjoy stability in office after a time of teaching and proven seriousness and performance in research and in other academic activities.

26. Oscar Arnulfo Romero was archbishop of San Salvador from 1976 to 1980, when he was assassinated during the Eucharistic celebration by a sniper.

the pastoral ministry derived from it, was found to reach only the elites; and also proposed a new program for the church. The second conference of the Latin American episcopate that took place in Medellín, Colombia, in 1968, had three main axes that made this program:

1. Faith and justice as an inseparable binomial of priorities;

2. A new way of doing theology, with one method: see/judge/act;

3. A new model of church starting from the articulation of community bases in poor regions, gathered around reading the Bible, and giving structure to the desire to be a church of the poor.[27]

The Latin American episcopal conference in Medellín became the first episcopal conference that, three years after the closing of Vatican II, officially responded to the call to read the signs of the times in the light of the Gospel.[28] It was also the first to make a "reception" of the council located in a non-European context.[29]

These points were confirmed at Puebla in 1979, already having behind them a decade of practice, results to evaluate, and background guidance to follow. The reception movement of Vatican II in the Latin American Church took root and created history. And these roots and this story had a tradition and specific names:

1. Preferential option for the poor

2. Liberation theology

3. Basic Ecclesial Communities

Liberation theology—a new structural approach to theology as a whole—came from the question: What does it mean to be a Christian on a continent of poor and oppressed people? At stake was a theology in line with the pastoral practice of a church that wanted to become freely poor, to stand with the poor, and to commit itself to the process of liberation from all forms of oppression and marginalization.

Moreover, this theology wanted to speak the language of indigenous and native cultures, evaluating their traditions, their rituals, and their modes of worship. This theology did not want to abolish those traditions

27. Bingemer, *Latin American Theology*.

28. Lassalle-Klein, *Blood and Ink*, 17.

29. Beozzo, "A recepção do Vaticano II na Igreja do Brasil"; Boff, "A recepção do Concílio Vaticano II no Brasil."

as simply non-Christian, but to respect them. Moreover, where these traditions and cultures lived together with the Christian culture brought about by colonial evangelization, efforts should be made to integrate them as a constitutive part of the church's discourse and praxis process. This would be, as the prominent Brazilian philosopher Henrique de Lima Vaz, SJ, said, our chance, as a Latin American church, to step outside this church that only projects and reflects the European church and theology and to approach a church that is a source of native and original living of the Gospel, thus generating a new way of thinking and talking about God, which is what it means to do theology.[30]

According to the definition from Peruvian priest and theologian Gustavo Gutiérrez, liberation theology is "a critical reflection on praxis."[31] However, it is Gutiérrez himself who claims that liberation theology does not start or depart from a simple critical analysis of reality. It begins with a mystical experience, a deep encounter with the Lord in the face of the poor. It also builds its system and speech with one method: see, judge, and act.[32] In an unfair and oppressive context there can be no theology without a social analysis of reality (SEE), which must subsequently be confronted with the Revelation present in Scripture (JUDGE). From these two moments should emerge a transformative strategy that guides and inspires the commitments and political positions of Christians (ACT).[33]

This theology—which started from a social analysis and praxis, before reaching reflection—could not only remain in books and academic courses, but should be returned to the poor to help them put their liberation process into action. Liberation theology wanted to strengthen the struggles of the poor to build a new society and fight with the poor so that they could be subjects of their own history.

30. Vaz, "Igreja reflexo vs. Igreja fonte," 17–22.

31. Gutiérrez, *Teología de la Liberación*, 32. However, Gustavo Gutiérrez distinguishes liberating praxis from historical praxis. For him, liberating praxis is "the process by which the faith of the Church builds or helps to build the spiritual and intellectual economic liberation of socially oppressed peoples as a fulfillment of the kingdom of God."

32. This method is due to the fierce French lay movement "Action Catholique" founded by Father Lebret. It was taken over and enriched by liberation theologians.

33. See also the great book on the Latin American theological method: C. Boff, *Teologia e Prática Teologia do Político e suas mediações*. The author follows the method of the French lay movement Action Catholique, using mediations of reality and biblical reading to build theological thought and discourse: socioanalytical mediation, hermeneutic mediation, and theological production.

After the council in Latin America, the term "option for the poor" was used by those who saw the church on the continent and must take up the cause of justice inseparably from the cause of the spread of faith.[34] The Episcopal Conferences of Medellín in 1968 and Puebla in 1979 confirmed at the level of the continent's episcopate this option as the option of the whole Latin American church.

The 1970s were very fertile and productive in the development of Latin American theology. Many initiatives have started and advanced steadily. A large number of bishops and religious authorities supported the option for the poor and the new theology that gave them voice. Pope Paul VI had some differences with liberation theology but never took initiatives against it.[35]

Many theological institutes and colleges had teachers who were inspired by liberation theology and taught its content. Many also participated in poor parishes over the weekend or even lived in poor regions such as the slums or "poblaciones," sharing the lives of the poor.[36] Clodovis Boff, for example, lived one semester in the far north of Brazil, in the state of Acre, working with the poor, and spent another semester teaching at the Pontifical Catholic University of Rio de Janeiro.[37]

The Basic Ecclesial Communities (CEBs) spread throughout the continent, especially in Brazil. It is estimated that in the 1980s its number reached approximately eighty thousand; the reason was that they were simpler and more horizontal in their way of being church, based on reading the Bible against social reality to produce transformative actions for the benefit of the poor.[38]

In 1978, John Paul II was elected pope. It was the beginning of a difficult time for liberation theologians. The new pontiff reigned twenty-six

34. According to the theologian Andrade, from PUC-Rio, the Spanish theologian J. Lois was the first to use the phrase "option for the poor." Lois, *Teología de la Liberación*.

35. He appointed many progressive bishops in Latin America during his pontificate, from 1963 to 1978, including Oscar Romero in El Salvador, and Bishop Helder Câmara in Brazil.

36. For example, the theologian Ronaldo Muñoz in Chile. Many Jesuits followed this path, such as Benjamin Gonzalez Buelta and Jorge Cela, who in the Dominican Republic had their first community experience in the Guachupita neighborhood. Buelta, *Bajar al encuentro de Dios*.

37. Boff taught at the Pontifical University of Rio de Janeiro until 1983, when he was banned from teaching theology by Cardinal Eugênio de Araújo Salles, due to his book *Teologia de pé no chão* (Down to Earth Theology).

38. Bingemer, *Latin American Theology*, 33.

years and his long pontificate was marked—among other things—by a negative understanding of what was going on in the Latin American church. The biggest difficulty for the new pope was that in using the see-judge-act method, many liberation theologians relied on Marxist categories of social analysis. The Vatican feared that socio-economic and political mediation would promote class struggle and adopt Marxist dialectical materialism as a privileged perspective for reading and interpreting history.[39]

The Polish pope, who was deeply committed to supporting the struggle in Eastern Europe (including the Solidarity [Solidarnosc] movement in Poland), did not see this reference to Marxist doctrine as a good thing. Nor did the Holy See. The discussion sharpened over the legitimacy of using Marxist categories to understand an oppressed and conflicting reality like that of Latin America. John Paul II, committed to ending communism in Eastern Europe, neither admitted nor understood how priests, bishops, nuns, and even laity could use a theology that relied onMarxist categories of analysis and openly and publicly supported political systems such as Cuba's, or the Sandinista Revolution in Nicaragua.[40]

The Vatican's dislike of liberation theology was expressed in two instructions, published in 1984 (*Libertatis Nuntius*) and 1986 (*Libertatis Conscientia*). The first was very critical; the second, a little less. During this period, however, liberation theology experienced several difficulties with the church hierarchy over its use of Marxist-oriented analysis.

What Rome seemed to have trouble understanding was that liberation theology intended to build a new way of doing theology and, even more, wanted to do it within the church. It was an academic proposition, but also a pastoral one. Those who embraced this option had a desire to take place within the church in the service of the poor to help them overcome their poverty and oppression. The most prominent theologians, who studied abroad for several years, rethought theological topics from the perspective of the poor, obtained diplomas, and wrote books and articles. However, none of them wanted to leave the church. There was

---

39. Govern, *Liberation Theology.*

40. One of the notable images of those years was that of Pope John Paul II arriving in Nicaragua and repressing Father Ernesto Cardenal, who served in the Sandinista government as minister of culture. He had knelt to receive the papal blessing when the pope addressed him irritably, ordering him to straighten out his situation with the Church. See also the biography of Ernesto's brother Fernando Cardenal, *Sacerdote em la revolución.*

no intention of forming a parallel church, or a "popular church," as the Vatican suspected.[41]

In 1989 this whole movement was strongly shaken by the fall of the Berlin Wall and the ensuing blow to the intrahistoric utopias that advocated for a transformation of grounded reality over a socialist and distributive model. The church was not immune to this impact. The new configuration of the Latin American church, which wanted to be a source church and not a projection church,[42] was considerably scattered and destroyed.

With the fall of "real socialism," there was a sudden shift in the path of the church of the continent toward the inseparability between justice and faith in the Gospel of Jesus. Neoliberalism as an ideology has grown.[43] Jesuit Provincials in Latin America wrote a letter criticizing it as a system in 1996.[44] But the same continued to grow. Liberation theology was strongly opposed during the pontificate of John Paul II. But this crisis has helped liberation theology resist and broaden the scope of its interests, which have become more global, including ecology, gender, race, ethnicity, and religious pluralism and interreligious dialogue.

However, the differences between north and south remained the same and even widened. The crisis in the north in 2008 made things worse for the south, and social justice is still a long way off and unreached. In this context we describe above the educational project of the UCA of El Salvador, which follows coherently the movement that forms the whole order of the Jesuits in Latin America. Within the perspective of the option for the poor and the centrality of the binomial faith and justice, educational institutions had to revise their premises, foundations, and configurations. UCA was a pioneer in this regard and inspired other institutions as well. At that university there was a project that strongly and socially included the issue of social justice as an integral part of teaching and research and the ideal of academic excellence that characterizes all the universities and especially the Jesuit universities.

41. Bingemer, *Latin American Theology*, 36. It brings more elements about this period and the conflictive discussion that marked it.

42. Cf. Vaz, "Igreja reflexo vs. Igreja fonte," 17–22. Cf. our book Bingemer, *Latin American Theology*.

43. Boff, "Igreja militante de Joao Paulo II," 87–111.

44. "Iglesia."

The Role of the Jesuits in the Post-Conciliar Latin American Movement

After Vatican II, Father Pedro Arrupe, SJ, was elected superior general of the Society of Jesus, the largest religious congregation of the Catholic Church in the world. In May 1968, he held a meeting with the largest Jesuit superiors of Latin America in Rio de Janeiro. The final document—known as the Rio Letter—was a policy statement for the Society of Jesus in light of the council, reconfiguring and rethinking its apostolate in each field. We can feel in this document the influence of Medellín's proposals:

> We seek to guide all our apostolate . . . to participate, as we can, in the common search of all people (whatever their ideology) for a freer, fairer and more peaceful society. We want the Society of Jesus to be actively present in the temporal life of humanity today: having as its sole criterion the Gospel message interpreted by the Church, without exerting any power in civil society and seeking no political purpose, merely wanting to shape the consciences of individuals and others of the communities. . . . Are we able to meet the expectations of the world? Do our faith and charity respond to the anxious appeal of the world around us? Do we practice self-denial sufficiently so that God can flood us with light and energy? Personal prayer has its own place in our lives so that we may be united with God in this great human task that cannot succeed without God?[45]

Father Arrupe, superior general of the Society of Jesus at the time of the second conference of the Latin American Episcopate in Medellín, Colombia, speaks of this option for the poor in a letter to the Jesuits of Latin America in 1968. And although the great stars of theological thought of this option, later called liberation theology, are the then-diocesan priest Gustavo Gutiérrez, now a member of the Order of Preachers, and the then-Franciscan friar Leonardo Boff, now a layperson, the Jesuits were present as a group, as a community, as a think tank, and were of fundamental help in spreading this theology throughout the continent that would be taught in seminaries and colleges of theology.[46]

---

45. Hennelly, *Liberation Theology*, 78–82.

46. We remember here with great memory the names of the great Jesuits committed to this project, such as João Batista Libanio from Brazil, Ricardo Antoncich from Peru, Victor Codina from Bolivia, Bartolomè Melià from Paraguay, Jon Sobrino from El Salvador, and many others.

The Jesuit meeting with Father Pedro Arrupe in Rio de Janeiro took place a few months before Medellín. And the results of this meeting played a major role in the history of the Jesuits of the Central American province and UCA, even inspiring the province's retreat in December 1969. The final document of the Rio meeting in 1968 will express the awareness of all Jesuits.

Their option for the poor has a political dimension. They themselves affirm: "We hope to participate, as best we can, in the common pursuit of all peoples . . . for a freer, fairer, and more peaceful society."[47] And they continue: "In all our activities, our goal would be to liberate humanity from every kind of bondage that oppresses it . . . aware of the profound transformation this presupposes . . . including a break with some of our past attitudes. It is almost certain that this will provoke reactions . . . but we promise to work for radical reforms that will radically transform existing structures (*Populorum Progressio* n. 32) . . . as the only way to promote social peace."[48]

The 1969 retreat will follow the itinerary of the *Spiritual Exercises of St. Ignatius*, seeking to apply Ignatian meditations and contemplations to the reality of the Latin American continent. Miguel Elizondo, who gave some of the retreat's lectures, says in proposing meditation on the kingdom of Christ[49] to the companions of the province: "the world will not be saved only through prayer or only through penance, but rather, in this Ignatian vision, through apostolic action which is at the same time prayer."[50]

In this project, many Jesuits were committed to insertion communities among the poor (Jesuit communities who no longer lived in schools or parishes or comfortable houses, but among the poor, sharing the way they lived with them). Others were committed to doing this new kind of theology that had the poor at its center.

That means that, while many engaged as individuals, the Society of Jesus engaged as an apostolic body. It was remarkable, the performance of the Jesuits in Latin America in those post-conciliar years in all fields: intellectual, pastoral, educational. There was an awareness on the part of the Society of Jesus and its superiors that it was necessary to answer the questions raised at the 1968 meeting in a concrete and patent manner.

Even if these questions were addressed to religious and consecrated men, such as the Jesuits, each Christian could take them as an invitation and

47. "Letter from Rio," quoted by Lassalle-Klein, *Blood and Ink*, 78–79.

48. "Letter from Rio," quoted by Lassalle-Klein, *Blood and Ink*, 78–79.

49. St. Ignatius of Loyola, *Spiritual Exercises*, n. 91–98.

50. Elizondo, "A visão inaciana do seguimento de Cristo," 1–8.

personal challenge. Christians living in a region like Latin America, marked by injustice and oppression, were called to respond in a special way. The '70s and '80s saw a lot of Latin American Christians very committed to this new way of being church and to think and propose faith in the God of Jesus Christ. And many lay Ignatian people formed by their works and institutes have made this choice in their lives and have become fervent defenders of the choice taken by the church as a whole in Medellín and Puebla.

The *Teologia e Libertação* collection, published at the same time in several languages and in many countries,[51] had a good group of Jesuits on its list of authors: João Batista Libanio, Xavier Albo, Bartolomé Meliá, Pedro Trigo, and the most well-known of the whole group, Jon Sobrino—professor at UCA of El Salvador—who wrote remarkable books rethinking Christology and ecclesiology from the victims' point of view. The concept of "victims" was coined by him as more inclusive than the poor viewed only from the socioeconomic-political perspective to name those who suffer under any form of injustice and violence.[52] The orientations of the Latin American church and the orientations of the Society of Jesus of those years went, therefore, in the same direction and reinforced each other.[53]

Father Peter-Hans Kolvenbach, successor of Father Arrupe as superior general of the Society of Jesus from 1983 to 2008, did not hesitate to say that "it was Latin America that opened the eyes of the Jesuits to preferential love for the poor and true and integral liberation as the priority perspective for the present mission of the Society of Jesus." And we can add: not only the eyes of the Jesuits, but also of many Christians around the world. The author of the book from which this quote was taken, a French journalist, rightly comments, "This was the beginning of a new phase in social Catholicism."[54]

With the fall of the Berlin Wall in 1989 and the movement of the world's balance of power, neoliberal capitalism floated triumphant. And the world has seen many of the utopias that presented another model of society toppled: more horizontal, egalitarian, where human rights have priority over enrichment, where sharing is more important than profit.

51. The books that came out were published in Portuguese, Spanish, English, German, and Italian. See these volumes that came out on the website of the publishing company Voices, responsible for publishing in Brazil: www.vozes.com.br.

52. Cf. his works: Sobrino, *Christology in Latin America*; and Sobrino, *Jesus in Latin America*.

53. Beirne, *Jesuit Education*, 52.

54. Antoine, *Le sang des justes*, 12.

The Jesuit provincials of Latin America jointly wrote a letter against neoliberalism in 1996, which was a reflection paper on this state of affairs. In it, they expressed the desire to concretely contribute to transforming the reality of society, creating "conditions for the possibility of fraternal coexistence through which Jesuit martyrs gave their lives in many parts of Latin America."[55]

The Educational Apostolate of the Society of Jesus in the Post-Conciliar Church

Ignacio Ellacuría as Dean of the UCA of El Salvador sought to apply the principles and ideals of the post-conciliar Latin American church by setting up a university model geared to the needs of the Salvadoran people.

Indeed, at UCA, in the project already inherited by Ellacuría and continued and perfected by him, the central concern is less with orthodoxy and pastoral attention to students than with attention and service to the dramatic issues of poverty and oppression in the country of El Salvador. It is not exactly a contradiction to Newman's proposal (knowledge as a value in itself) or that of Pope John Paul II in the apostolic constitution *Ex Corde Ecclesiae* (the university as a means of evangelization).[56] It is above all a difference of emphasis, but one that is crucial in shaping the face of the university, concerned more with the urgencies of social justice than with theological orthodoxy. This explains why UCA has always insisted on preserving its autonomy in the face of eventual dependence on not only civil but also religious and ecclesiastical authorities of its time and place.[57]

The source of this conception also lies in the evolution itself in the understanding of education by the Society of Jesus. Father Arrupe, elected general of the order after the council, at the meeting with the provincial superiors in Rio de Janeiro in 1968, signals the adherence of the Society to the ecclesial movement begun in Medellín. The final document—which we have already quoted here—is a statement of the Society of Jesus's principles in light of the council, reconfiguring and rethinking its apostolate in all areas.

---

55. Ivern, *O neoliberalismo da América Latina.* This document provoked strong reactions from conservative sectors of society. See article by Economy Minister Roberto Campos, "O neobobismo dos jesuítas."

56. Pope Francis, *Veritatis Gaudium* (2018).

57. Beirne, *Jesuit Education,* 40.

"We intend to direct the totality of our apostolate . . . to participate, as best we can, in the common search of all peoples (whatever their ideology) for a freer, fairer, and more peaceful society. We wish the Society of Jesus to be present in the temporal life of humanity today: having as its sole criterion the gospel message as interpreted by the church, exercising no power in civil society, and seeking nonpolitical goals, seeking only to form the consciences of individuals and communities."[58]

From this total commitment of the Society, there were some points addressed directly to the Jesuit universities in Latin America: "We promise to work for consistent reforms that will radically transform existing structures . . . promote social peace. . . . The integration of social life into the Christian lifestyle calls for a theological and philosophical reflection that addresses the whole world and its pressing problems."[59]

The Rio Letter continued, talking now about the new phase in which this whole educational project was entering. "Education, for example, is a major factor in social change. We think it is more important for our schools and universities to accept their role as active agents of national integration and social justice in Latin America. We will not have development for all until we have comprehensive education for all. . . . First and foremost we must instill an attitude of service to society in all our students and a genuine concern for marginal groups. Our students must participate in the transformation of today's society and in the work of improving the human condition."[60]

The provincials ended their document with provocative questions for the Jesuits in Latin America.[61] And these questions will equally be addressed to all those—Jesuits or religious or lay collaborators—who were working in the universities under the responsibility of the Society of Jesus.

Here we see the whole ideal of St. Ignatius, which was defined by his secretary Polanco as "a contemplative in action." This was also the profile of Father Arrupe, a visionary and mystic who, being a novice master in Japan, did not hesitate to turn the novitiate into a hospital to treat those injured by the bombs of Hiroshima and Nagasaki. Under his leadership and inspired by his prophetic vision aligned with the council's impulse, the

58. Compañía de Jesús. "Reunión," n. 78.

59. Compañía de Jesús. "Reunión," n. 79.

60. Compañía de Jesús. "Reunión," n. 80–81. Cf. above the text of these questions, inserted by us in the previous item.

61. Compañía de Jesús. "Reunión," n. 82.

Jesuits of Latin America dreamed of turning their apostolic works toward the liberation and promotion of the continent's poor. The consequences of this option will be felt. In the Society of Jesus of this post-conciliar age, there is a growing commitment to the poor and the oppressed. The mysticism generated by this commitment is ardent and beautiful. There are even many who wish to share with the poor, to some extent, the effects of injustice and oppression in order to collaborate in the liberation process that they themselves wanted to undertake.[62]

After this meeting in Rio de Janeiro, the Jesuits had another meeting that had a great impact on the future of UCA: the 32nd General Congregation of the Order, held in Rome in 1972, and which has a statute of authority within the Society of Jesus.

The focal point of this General Congregation was the question and answer in the decree "Jesuits Today": "What does it mean to be a companion of Jesus today? It is to engage, under the banner of the Cross, in the crucial struggle of our time: the struggle for faith, of which the struggle for justice is a constitutive part."[63]

These words are inscribed on a bronze plaque on the tomb of the UCA Jesuits who were murdered in 1989 in the garden of their house where their community lived. A chapel was built there respecting even part of the garden.[64] This tribute means the recognition that this particular community has led to the ultimate consequences of this commitment and lifestyle. This consisted in the synthesis of the UCA project. Ignacio Ellacuría received a university already turned toward the social context in which it was inserted and continued to promote this way of conceiving and leading this institution by applying to it the orientations of the church in Latin America and also the mysticism and the intuitions and inspirations of the religious order itself.

This inscription speaks louder than anyone about UCA's self-understanding of its own identity. The university saw its Christian inspiration rooted in specific commitments to the poor rather than in canonical legal control and explicitly religious practices. And it was at the same time critical of the other Jesuit universities, which were more concerned with religious issues than with the urgencies of the vast majority of the

---

62. Pedro Arrupe, opening remarks to the Congregation of prosecutors, in Calvez, *Foi et justice*, 56, quoted by Antoine, *Le sang des justes*.

63. General Congregation 32, Decree 4.

64. Beirne, *Jesuit Education*, 52.

population—the poor. The Center for Theological Reflection at the university was an effective instrument for UCA to carry out its mission from the 1970s. This Pastoral Center Monsignor Romero, as well as the theological library, with the publication of the journals *Carta a las Iglesias* and *Revista Latino-Theology*, as well as academic programs ranging from pastoral institutes to master's studies, were seen by the university staff as contributing to the country's religious life.

With more Jesuit students studying at UCA and assisting in lay ministry, the university has become a center of religious renewal and formation, earning the admiration of the most progressive sectors of the church and the suspicion of the more traditional. To this day, UCA's theology course attracts students not only from the country, but also lay Christians from the northern hemisphere who want to dive into the suffering Latin American reality.

It was, therefore, clear to the UCA community that religious commitment was not separate from that of social transformation. It is in the dynamic interaction of these two poles, therefore, that Christian inspiration of the university was clear and guaranteed.

This also ensured persecution and risk. Solidarity with the poor and the fight for justice were considered attacks on state security, frequently punishable by death. And this has happened in many countries, especially in Central America (Nicaragua, Guatemala, and El Salvador from UCA) but also in the Southern Cone (Argentina, Chile, and Brazil). The extreme right that felt threatened by the positions taken by the church and, in particular, by the Jesuits, manifested itself with international support in the most belligerent terms.

An example of this is the document from the Latin American Anticommunist Confederation (CAL), established in 1972 as a branch of the Cold War civil organization, the World Anticommunist League (WACL), which denounces "the participation of the Jesuit clergy in the Marxism of the youth in El Salvador . . . in Christian colleges, universities, or communities . . . 'and explicitly proposing' . . . the immediate expulsion of these Marxist Jesuits and thus, by this example, to administer the proof that our Christian anticommunism is incompatible with his 'liberation theology.'"[65]

Moreover, in the media of various countries in Latin America, Europe, and the United States, the lie spread that Rutilio Grande had left his

---

65. Antoine, *Le sang des justes,* 80–81. Sobrino and Ellacuría are mentioned in the text.

religious community to become a "guerrillero."[66] The motto *Haga patria mate un cure* (Be patriotic, kill a priest) was spread on posters all over the capital San Salvador.

Father Arrupe gives all his support to his Jesuits. He will spell out this support when he comes to attend the Third Conference of the Latin American Episcopate in Puebla, Mexico, in 1979. He gives an interview and statement when asked about death threats against the Jesuits in El Salvador. Arrupe replies that he himself asked his Jesuits to stay in El Salvador. Withdrawal would be a demonstration of fear and this would be incompatible with the charism of the order because, according to Arrupe, "the Society of Jesus does not allow itself to be threatened."[67]

In fact, by turning the educational institution that the university was entirely toward the goal of liberating the poor of El Salvador, UCA was just following a centuries-old tradition, not only Jesuit but also ecclesial. From the first moment of the gospel's arrival in America—with the evangelizing project united with the colonial project, not recognizing the value of the native peoples' indigenous cultures and later enslaving thousands of Africans torn from their lands to be sold as merchandise—voices denounced this attitude and this state of affairs. Prophetism has never been absent from ecclesial practice in Latin America.[68]

What is unique about the UCA project is the fact that it is setting up an entire higher education institution that should normally be pursuing academic excellence as a priority, pursuing funding to obtain awards and to gain worldwide recognition, and training professionals who would occupy various positions. For government and leadership in the various aspects of society, UCA would mean something else: justice and the liberation of the poorest who constituted and still constitute the overwhelming majority of the peoples of the country and of the continent where the university is located.

66. Antoine, *Le sang des justes*, 81. Pope Francis shed light on this insidious doubt by unleashing the process of canonization of Rutilius and beatifying him on January 22, 2022.

67. Calvez, *Foi et justice*, 69.

68. Cf. the well-known and important performances of figures such as Bartolome de Las Casas, Antonio de Montesinos, Francisco de Vitoria, and others.

UCA: A University at the Service of Social Transformation

It is important to make clear that the Jesuits' commitment to the fight for justice is not entirely new. In the southern hemisphere, and particularly in southern America, the Jesuits, since the early years of the founding of the Society of Jesus, have been engaged in evangelical work for a more just world, even if the settings of this appointment may have varied from place to place and context to context.

In the seventeenth and eighteenth centuries, some more lucid Jesuits defended the native populations from the conquerors, slave hunters.[69] The Guarani reductions of the New World, true self-managed and economically and culturally prosperous cities for over a century, are absolutely due to the prophetic vision and the firm hand of the Jesuits.[70]

There is no need to forget about the performance of other Jesuits in Latin America in responding to other social and political challenges of their time, even if these challenges included religious issues. As an example, we can cite the great Antonio Vieira, considered by many to be "the emperor of the Portuguese language," who tirelessly defended the Jews and new Christians in Brazil against the Inquisition.[71]

This greatness was also the source of countless conflicts, misunderstandings, and persecutions suffered over time: suppression, expulsion, etc. What happened, therefore, in the same southern hemisphere, specifically in Central America in the second quarter of the twentieth century, was only a continuation of this tradition. And as it turned out, the motto that united the service of faith and the promotion of justice epitomized something that the Society of Jesus had already done and continued to do on the continent, but that gained new momentum and strength with the Second Vatican Council and the choices of the Latin American Church, with the conferences of Medellín and Puebla.

The government of Father Pedro Arrupe, as superior general of the society, who had supported, as we have seen, initiatives of Latin American Jesuits such as Ellacuría and the UCA community, concretely made the choice for the binomial faith and justice practiced deeply and radically by many Jesuits on the continent. Gradually, a stronger and more radical

69. Souza, "Las Casas," 25–59.

70. Melià and Nagel, *Guaraníes y Jesuítas*, 306.

71. Paiva, *Padre Antonio Vieira*; Besselaar, *Antônio Vieira*.

concrete application of the union of faith with the practice of justice began to become clearer and more evident.

And this happens in a privileged way in a small country, a lost point in Central America: the country that bears the name of Jesus Christ, the Savior, a name inherited from the conquerors who arrived there sponsored by the most majestic Christian Isabella the Catholic, Queen of Castile. El Salvador is a small country with six million inhabitants and a surface area that is half the size of Switzerland. The social inequalities in the period when the Jesuit assassinations took place in the UCA are stark. In El Salvador, 70 percent of the land belongs to 1 percent of the population and 90 percent of the peasants have no land to cultivate. Commitment and preferential treatment of the poor will cost the Jesuits the price of their blood.

Beyond these inequalities, El Salvador was a strategic point for the United States, which was defending Western and Christian civilization in the name of the world offensive against communism. In the 1970s we were in the midst of the Cold War between the West and the royal socialism of the Soviet Union. Fidel Castro's Cuba was an exception throughout America, when the southern armies joined the north in the systematic and continuous pursuit of anything that might even resemble communism.

In the Southern Cone there were booming military dictatorships that went down in history as bloody decimaters of leftist militants, including many Christians and Catholics, such as Pinochet's Chile, Videla's Argentina, and Brazil of the many generals who were noted for the torture learned at the School of the Americas.[72]

In these countries above all, many Catholics who engaged under so-called left-wing banners were persecuted by the military regimes of force. And the cause of the poor and their commitment to it meant that, in the eyes of the conservative, elitist, militarized right, Marxism, materialism,

---

72. The Western Hemisphere Institute for Security Cooperation, also known by its former name, Schoool of the Americas, is a United States Army military education organization located in Fort Benning, in the US city of Columbus, Georgia. The school was in operation from 1946 to 1984 in the Panama Canal Zone, where since 2000 the Meliá Panamá Canal Hotel has been operating. More than 60,000 military and police officers from up to twenty-three Latin American countries have graduated, some of them of special relevance for crimes against humanity, such as officers Leopoldo Fortunato Galtieri, Omar Torrijos, Manuel Antonio Noriega, Manuel Contreras, and Vladimiro Montesinos. Certain sources ("Escuela de las Américas" and "La escuela de las Américas: EEUU entrena terroristas") denounced that this place "has trained methods of torture, murder, and repression to thousands of repressors from all over Latin America." This activity continues to this day. Cf. "Instituto del Hemisferio."

and communism could no longer be distinguished from evangelical commitment to social justice. Thus it was the far-right Catholics in El Salvador—and in other Latin American countries such as the Southern Cone mentioned above—that unleashed a wave of violence rarely seen against Christians who advocated a more social line.

At the same time, there were church figures, especially bishops, who were able to raise their voices without brutally silencing those who spoke and took a stand to denounce torture and injustice, condemn the violence committed in the name of preserving privileges, and put themselves to rest with the poor against the forces of repression. Noteworthy and worth remembering in the Southern Cone are Brazilians Dom Helder Câmara, Dom Paulo Evaristo Arns, Dom Ivo Lorscheiter, Dom Antonio Fragoso, Dom Pedro Casaldáliga, and many others. Also in Argentina, Monsignor Angelelli, who ended up dead in an ambiguous car accident. Monsignor Angelelli is in the process of being canonized and is considered a martyr at the Vatican.[73] And in Chile, also worth remembering are Cardinal Silva, Monseñor Manuel Larrain, many Jesuits, and the whole institution of Vicaría de la Solidaridad.[74]

In El Salvador the conflict took on the aspect of open warfare, even though the regime was not officially considered a dictatorship. Among the many great figures in the country who suffered the violent repression of those who defended their interests and opposed any change were "thousands of members of basic ecclesial communities, catechists, popular militants, priests, religious, etc. It was a war theoretically against communism, but in fact defending the political and economic interests of its protagonists. The Jesuits denounced this: "The climate of anxiety and collective panic is not only the fruit of the country's decaying and pernicious structures; it is also the result of insulting and slandering campaigns, blindness by some, as well as the senseless violence unleashed against them, the small, and against all who truly seek to serve the people, whether they are priests or religious, peasants or intellectuals. Fear reigns today throughout society."[75]

Amid this climate of fear and dread that produced countless victims of these conflicts, some figures stood out for their courage, for the clarity

---

73. Álvarez, "Enrique Angelelli."

74. About Chile, see "Jorge Houston, hoje afastado"; About Brazil, see Serbin, *Diálogos na Sombra*; Mainwaring, *Igreja Católica e Política no Brasil*; About Argentina, see "Bergoglio e o papel da Igreja na ditadura argentina."

75. Antoine, *Le sang des justes*, 58.

of their evangelical witness and for their heroic martyrdom: Jesuit Rutilio Grande, a pioneer of Catholic renewal in the countryside, shot down while on his way to Aguilares in the company of two of his parishioners, a young man and an elderly man.[76] On March 12, 1977, Father Rutilio—accompanied by Manuel Solorzano, 72, and Nelson Rutilio Lemus, 16—drove the Jeep given to him by Archbishop Oscar Romero on the road between the city of Aguilares and the municipality of El Paísnal to celebrate the Mass of St. Joseph's novena, when the three were ambushed and murdered by death squads.

Upon learning of the murders, Monsignor Oscar Romero, who was a friend of Father Rutilio, went to the place where the three bodies were and celebrated Mass. Then Romero spent several hours listening to local farmers, learning their personal stories of suffering. He also spent hours in prayer. The next morning, after meeting with the priests and counselors, Romero said he would not participate in any joint activities with the government and the president until their deaths were investigated. As no investigation was made, Monsignor Oscar Romero no longer attended any state ceremony during his three years as archbishop.

Monsignor Oscar Arnulfo Romero, archbishop of San Salvador, had a conservative and moderate profile as bishop and was therefore appointed to assume the primary seat of the country as archbishop of San Salvador. His generous and evangelical heart, however, was so impacted by the testimony and death of his great friend Rutilio Grande that he pledged himself to supporting the poor, denouncing injustice and violence, and using the homilies he pronounced with his powerful and prophetic voice heard every Sunday. He ended up being the object of the hatred of conservative groups and was shot to death in the midst of the celebration of the Eucharist. Monsignor Romero was canonized in 2018.[77]

A group of four American women, three nuns, Maura Clarke, Ita Ford (both sisters of the Maryknoll congregation), and Dorothy Kazel

76. Rutilio Grande García was a Jesuit priest from El Salvador, born on July 5, 1928, in El Paísnal (El Salvador), where he also died, murdered, on March 12, 1977. As a result of his murder, Archbishop Oscar Romero began to demand that the government investigate the crime. This process would change the way Romero saw the relationship between church and politics.

77. The beatification process of Father Rutilio had its diocesan phase completed in 2014 and from there went to Rome. Rutilio Grande was beatified on January 22, 2022. See "Padre Rutilio Grande" and "O Papa quer." Rutilio Grande was canonized already by Pope Francis.

(Ursulina), and a laywoman (Jennifer Donovan) who worked in pastoral care with the poor in El Salvador, were attacked on their return from the airport, raped, and killed a few months after the assassination of Monsignor Romero on December 2, 1980.

The community of the six Jesuits who made up the UCA residence was the dean and five others, as well as two women who worked at home, a mother and daughter. The whole community was shot down at dawn, when it was dark and there were no witnesses, by an elite Salvadoran army battalion. Father Jon Sobrino, also a member of that community, escaped the massacre because he was in Thailand teaching a theology course.

With the martyrdom of this whole community began a new stage in the history of the Society of Jesus in America.[78] The memory of the martyrs was an inspiration to the Society of Jesus and to the church and also to other people and institutions outside the church.[79]

Within the community stood the figure of the president of the university: philosopher, theologian, and brilliant thinker, political negotiator, and conflict mediator, Ignacio Ellacuría. He, who was already a prominent person on the whole issue of liberation theology and the option for the poor in Latin America, had now, illuminated by his martyrdom, considerably increased credibility. His companion and friend Jon Sobrino says: "Ellacuría . . . had the gift of letting reality speak. Ellacuría did what he did not just because he had an idea, but because he was driven by reality. . . . If we look back, however . . . and ask what helped him conceptualize this reality, it was Zubiri and Rahner."[80] In Ellacuría's personality, therefore, were the roots that made him intellectually and spiritually what he was: a philosopher disciple of Zubiri, a theologian inspired by Karl Rahner's theology, and a Jesuit formed by the *Spiritual Exercises of St. Ignatius of Loyola.*

Also in the same community were others who made brilliant contributions to university thought and knowledge on the Latin American continent. Jon Sobrino, along with Ellacuría, created theological reflections that developed with depth and consistency Latin American theology and made it known throughout the world. To this day he is one of the great Latin American theologians, along with Gustavo Gutiérrez and others. Doctoral

78. Antoine, *Le sang des justes,* 13.

79. Cf. the thinker Noam Chomsky who has in his office a photo of the six Jesuit martyrs and has great admiration for them. Vitoria, "Chomsky, Romero."

80. Jon Sobrino, in interviews with Robert Lassalle-Klein, cited in Lassalle-Klein, *Blood and Ink,* 185.

theses on his work abound, both in Brazil and abroad.[81] Ignacio Martin Baró attracted international interest with his "liberation psychology," which was discussed, welcomed, and prestigious at academic congresses in the US, Europe, and Latin America.[82]

The project led by Ellacuría was to try to "do in our way of being university what Monsignor Romero did in his way of being pastoral."[83] With his option to return to the university for the national reality of the country, UCA had academic programs and publications that reflected and argued about it. Magazines like *American Studies (ECA)*, *Latin American Journal of Theology*, *proceso*, *letter to Las Iglesias*, and others interacted with areas such as law, communication, administration, economics, and psychology. The professors and researchers of the UCA collaborated on projects such as the "Vivienda minima," which were housing cooperatives at low cost.

Ellacuría was in constant dialogue with national leaders of several lines, both at home and abroad, from the leader of the farabundo Martí Liberation Front National (FMLN) to the Ambassador of the United States. According to Montes, he traveled the whole country studying its basic social structures and human rights violations, talking to the people who suffered these realities in their own flesh.[84] Ignacio Martin Barò conducted opinion polls, so that the people of El Salvador could make public their feeling about the things that were going on there, since there is no voice in the public organizations. And he was doing his psychological research. Jon Sobrino reflected on all this reality theologically. And this is how it inaugurated new areas within Latin American theology, introducing concepts such as Christology from the victims, theology as *Intellectus Amoris* more than *Intellectus fidei*, etc.[85]

---

81. See Jon Sobrino's works in the bibliography to this book.

82. Ignacio Martín-Baró, a Jesuit and former vice dean of UCA, was murdered at forty-seven, and had no time to glimpse the directions his research on liberation psychology might take. He advocated a psychology of his own for each country that interacted with the ways of survival of the excluded. His legacy, twenty years after the martyrdom, remains in force, says Sol Yañez, coordinator of the Martín-Baró International Forum, in an interview given by email to IHU On-Line. "He went deeper into the study of groups, psychosocial trauma and encouraged the creation of knowledge networks, social networks and actions in favor of a liberating psychology," he says. Sol Yañez is a teacher at Universidad Centroamericana José Simeón Cañas de El Salvador (UCA). See the complete biography of Ignacio Martín-Baró at "Ignacio Martín-Baró (1942–1989)."

83. Ellacuría, *La UCA ante el doctorado concedido a Monseñor Romero*, 104.

84. Beirne, *Jesuit Education*, 232.

85. See his works at "Jon Sobrino."

Thus, several of them—according to Montes, Ignacio Martín-Baró, Amando Lopes, and Rodolfo Cardenal—combined their academic activities with pastoral presence and activity outside the university in poor parishes. The contact with the simplest people personally enriched them and reminded them day after day, week after week, the first and fundamental reason for which they did research, gave lessons, and administered the university: to transform an unfair and cruel reality toward the poor. Thus, in his pastoral and priestly action, the parishes and poor communities of the country and the classrooms and the university auditors were dynamically related to each other; they were mutually enriched and interdependent. It didn't make sense of one thing without the other. As knowledge progressed and deepened, his pastoral care became more fruitful and his mystical more consistent and profound. On its horizon was also the formation of future generations. Students were also put in touch with reality to be transformed and this did a huge good for their study and their formation. His talents were used to solve problems of education, housing, defense of human rights, and public health.[86]

Cesar Jerez, SJ, a Guatemalan who was Provincial Jesuit of Central America from 1976 to 1982 and 1984 to 1991, and dean of the Central American University of Managua (Nicaragua), recalls that "the third world university must commit itself in the context in which she lives. She must dwell on reality. . . . A Third-Worldist reality of growing poverty that cries out to the heavens and sustains its victims. . . . An impoverished society does not cease, however, to have enormous wealth and greater cultural potential."[87]

Ignacio Ellacuría: Philosopher, Theologian, and Dean of UCA

Within this community context appears the leadership of Ellacuría. As has been seen here, Ignacio Ellacuría was a Jesuit priest, philosopher, and theologian who did an important job as professor and dean of the Centro Universidad Americana "José Simeón Cañas" (UCA) founded in 1965. His

---

86. According to Rafael De Sivatte, current director of the department of theology at UCA, Ellacuría never accepted to have a medical school, despite having funding offered from foreign institutions to do so. Their reason was that as soon as doctors began to graduate there, the brightest and best would be immediately captured with tempting offers of millionaire salaries in the northern hemisphere and would not serve the country. Therefore, only the public health and sanitation course was implemented.

87. Jerez, "Speech of the UCA Dean."

work was decisive in the way that UCA took in its early years and subsequent years. Ellacuría was also responsible for developing training programs for Jesuit priests and students of Central America.

Ellacuría's academic work was an important contribution to the "Philosophy of Liberation." This school of philosophy is rooted in the work of Augusto Salazar Bondy (1925–74) and Leopoldo Zea (1912–2004). Its objective interest is the liberation of the oppressed in order to "reach the fullness of humanity." Ellacuría was also a strong supporter and collaborator of liberation theology. The political implications of Ellacuría's commitment to his ideas met with strong opposition from conservative religious and political forces in El Salvador. This opposition led to his assassination by the Salvadoran army in 1989 at his UCA residence along with five other fellow Jesuit priests and two women who worked at the residence, mother and daughter. His assassination marked a turning point in the Salvadoran civil war. On the one hand, it increased international pressure from the Salvadoran government to sign peace agreements with the guerrilla organization FMLN. On the other hand, it helped to make Ellacuría's ideas (hitherto known only in Latin America and Spain) known worldwide.

There are different types of Latin American liberation philosophy. The thought of Ellacuría represents one of the currents within this philosophical tradition. It claimed to be the inevitably personal, social, and historical human reality. Biology and society are elements of history, meaning they are always in motion. But this should not be confused with historical materialism, which says that human beings are passive instruments of historical forces. Human beings certainly inherit constraints built in the past, but always have the possibility of transcending them because of their intelligence.

Praxis is the name that Ellacuría gives to reflective human action, directed to the transformation of reality.[88] Unlike other animals that can only respond mechanically to stimuli from outside, through intelligence and praxis, humans have to "realize" their existence. Individuals in dialectical interaction with society must be able to decipher what kind of ego they have using their intelligence, and this implies transcending inherited constraints. This means that progress actually happens through a combination of physical, biological, and "praxic" factors. Through praxis, humans are able to realize a wide scope of action possibilities. In other words, praxis

88. In the same way this action is called by all Latin American liberation theology. Gustavo Gutiérrez introduced this category as central to liberation theology and other theologians, such as Clodovis Boff, who used it abundantly in his work.

can lead to a broader and more complete way of life. When this happens, praxis can be said to increase freedom if freedom is understood as movement to acquire greater possibilities for action.

According to Ellacuría, the existence of people who are marginalized by society implies that history and practice have not yet manifested a wider range of achievement possibilities for every human being in the world. This has prevented excluded people from realizing their existence as human beings. Therefore, there is a situation that remains far from the fullness of humanity and the fullness of reality. But this situation can be changed. For him, before the evolution of humanity, the further development of historical reality has already taken place only by physical and biological forces. But since the development of human beings, praxis can also contribute to realizing historical reality. Since human beings have the possibility to reflect, it is the philosopher's duty to exercise this ability to reflect in order to transform reality and allow greater possibilities for individual fulfillment.

Ellacuría intended to build a new theology, which he called historical theology. By historical theology he meant a way of doing theology: reflect on the faith from the historical present and reflect on the historical present from the faith. According to him, all theology is conditioned by its historical present. Historical theology intends to gain awareness of its historical context and to incorporate it fully. The concept of *locus theologicus* is very important in this theology. Following Ellacuría's thought, then, liberation theology would be seen as a new way of doing historical theology, in a particular *locus theologicus*: the historical present of Latin America, where a large portion of the population is oppressed by structures that deny the possibility to meet their needs and develop. It springs from the spirit of *Gaudium et Spes*, the Vatican Council II, and the social encyclicals of Pope John XXIII, and, more specifically, of the Episcopal Conferences of Medellín, Colombia, in 1968, and of Puebla, Mexico, in 1979.

"In Ellacuría one can find a liberation theologian writing about human salvation in history without collapsing the divine within the human."[89] According to Ellacuría, salvation is fulfilled historically, not only individually but collectively, and it should not be understood only as liberation from evil, guilt, personal or social offenses, pain, disease, and fetishism. These forms of liberation begin only after liberation from unjust structures such as slavery, political domination, or psychological and social oppression. But what makes Ellacuría a paradigmatic case, which

89. Lee, "Liberation Theology's Transcendent Moment," 226.

continues to challenge the understanding of the work of the Society of Jesus and the church in the south of the world today, is that he was president of a university and from that "locus" tried to do something that would appeal to the entire earth. From north to south, his actions will even be very suitable for the whole pastoral care of the church, as they treat and include includes many aspects of it.

The path Ellacuría followed about reality in his article "El desafío de las mayorías pobres," published in 1989, retains a thrilling currentness: his analysis (which he used to call coproanalysis, because he studies the scum of our civilization) reveals that this living system, this socioeconomic model, is seriously ill. The purpose of your analysis is precisely to bring a reflective line that avoids this fatal outcome. Because of this, he proposes to reverse the story, subvert it, and toss it in another direction, doing this together with all the world's poor and oppressed in a way that avoids every easy way to do it: utopically and hopefully.

Ellacuría was also a theologian and has a theological thought process that is very important to understanding his work as leader of the UCA. This coincided with the radical renewal that the Latin American church and theology were having during these years when he took over as dean.

This is where the UCA community gains surprising importance. The mass murder of the whole community and the gallows that have come to bear this martyrdom can help us understand and be enlightened by this communal martyrdom. It can also clarify the reasons why the UCA community and particularly Ellacuría questioned so much the military and oppressive government of El Salvador that it concluded they had to eliminate that community, as it had already done with Monsignor Romero; with the North American religious women Maura Clarke, Ita Ford, Dorothy Kazel, and the young laywoman Jean Donovan; and with so many others. Indeed, the background of this conflict lies in the philosophical and theological concepts that Ellacuría handles with impressive intellectual dexterity and that have shaped the entire community.

The Salvation of and in History

One of Ellacuría's most interesting counter-direction proposals lies in the idea of building a civilization of poverty. This proposal has to do with the dictatorship of consumerism and the civilization of welfare. To avoid misunderstanding, he explains his terms very clearly: "The civilization of poverty is thus called as opposed to the civilization of wealth and not because it seeks universal pauperization as an ideal of life. . . . What we want to underline here is the relationship dialectic richness-poverty in itself. In a world sinfully shaped by the dynamism of capital and wealth, it is necessary to raise and propose a different dynamism that surpasses it salvifically."[90]

Besides being a rigorous intellectual, Ellacuría also has a prophetic look at reality. It deals with the issues that are already burning and clearly defy thinking, as well as anticipating questions that will only emerge later. Today we see that to this sinful socioeconomic reality, shaped by a system that bets on profit at any cost, has been added an ever-clearer awareness of the consequences of this system on the devastation of the planet. The ecological crisis is not a distant ingredient, but an additional consequence of this predatory process, which, seeking insatiable consumerism and producing an unlimited amount of goods destined to satisfy immediate consumerist anxieties, leads to an unyielding unsustainability due to the disastrous ecological traces it leaves, ultimately putting the human race at an undoubted risk of extinction.[91]

Ellacuría argues that it is necessary to return to the primary goods: adequate nutrition, minimal right to housing, basic health care, primary education, and sufficient employment. For him, the great pending task is that all people can and should have decent access to the satisfaction of these needs, not as crumbs falling from the table of the rich, but as a fundamental part of the table of humanity. In his own words:

> This poverty is the one that really gives room to the spirit, which had not been stifled by the lustful urge to possess all sorts of superfluities, when most of humanity is lacking the basics it needs. Then the spirit will be able to flourish, the enormous spiritual and human wealth of the poor and Third World peoples, now drowned by misery and the imposition of more developed cultural models in some respects, but not because they are more fully human.[92]

90. "Utopía y profetismo," 170–75.

91. At this point we can say that Ellacuría, already in the '70 and '80s, is prophetic in relation to the ecological alert that today has become a primordial item in the universal agenda. And even on the ecclesial agenda, as Pope Francis' recent encyclical *Laudato Si'* shows.

92. "Misión actual de la Compañía de Jesús," 119–23.

Ellacuría wrote his text "Misión Actual de la Compañía de Jesús—La civilización de la pobreza"[93] as a contribution to the 33rd General Congregation of the Order in 1983. The content, in a rigorous and academic language, has the same accents as the decrees that will be adopted. "Poverty, writes the UCA Dean of San Salvador, "is a historic necessity and not just a council of perfection."[94]

However, for Ellacuría, this poverty is Jesuit and Christological, because

> she introduces a new civilization of austerity, perfectly ordered to the preaching of Jesus. A civilization of sharing, communicating goods and lives, human creativity as a flowering of inner grace. A civilization open to transcendence and particularly to the Christian form of transcendence as it was revealed in Jesus of Nazareth, he who made himself equal to the poorest to bring God's glory to a new view. Essential virtues such as self-denial, the gift of self, and hope in God, humility, love, etc., would find in this civilization of poverty the ground prepared for the abundant seeds to grow one by one, sown by the disciples of Jesus.[95]

Him and the entire UCA Jesuit community will seal with their blood this religious, Jesuit, Christian identity that marked their life and work.

An Intellectual Life at the Service of the Poor

There is no doubt that Ellacuría is an intellectual, and a brilliant intellectual. As a Jesuit, he has fifteen years of training and study, always with the best and most enthusiastic acknowledgments of his trainers and teachers. His greatest influence was that of the Spanish philosopher Xavier Zubiri. The proximity to Zubiri's philosophy puts him close to the most real part of reality, from which he will develop a praxis ethic that will open him to immense possibilities.

Ellacuría can write as a philosopher, but also as a theologian who welcomes human salvation in history without dissolving the divine in the human because he bases his theological reflections on the philosophical writings of his mentor, the Basque philosopher Xavier Zubiri, whose

93. Ellacuría, "Carta a las Iglesias," n. 297–99 (posthumous publication).
94. Ellacuría, "Carta a las Iglesias," n. 297–99.
95. Ellacuría, "Carta a las Iglesias," n. 297–99

main work concerns the human being and his intellection within reality.[96] Briefly summarizing the philosopher's thinking, Zubiri thinks God is not transcendent in relation to things, but rather God is transcendent "in" and "within" things.[97] Therefore, in relinking—a term he coined—human beings are open to things and find themselves among themselves and with them, but this is not the case when it comes to God. In relinking, human beings are not with God in a confession of faith, but rather with God because they adhere to good. They do not go toward God, but come from God (every going to is a being carried by God).[98] Thus, Zubiri will state that "we are led to understand not what" is, but what "makes it."[99]

Thus, Zubiri's understanding of God in relinking does not result in a distant mode of existence between God and the human being. But the Basque philosopher's view sees the future as the time when human beings "will find themselves reconnected with God, not just flying out of the world, and from others, and from themselves; but on the contrary, in order to sustain and maintain themselves in being."[100]

Ignacio Ellacuría is a follower and someone inspired by the thought of Zubiri. He began working with the philosopher in the 1960s. It was Zubiri—according to Michael Lee—who intensified Ellacuría's desire to bring to his theological work a genuine encounter with reality and to make this theological work address El Salvador's tragic reality.[101] Perhaps the focal point of Zubiri's influence on Ellacuría's contextual thinking rooted in El Salvador's disfigured reality lies in the fact that both the theologic and the theological are not the same thing. Zubiri analyzes reality by stating a description of God not as an object within reality, but as the foundation of reality.[102] And this, for both, is the theological dimension of reality. Human beings realize the weight of this reality that imposes itself on them. That is the power of the real.

96. See the premium work of Zubiri in three volumes of *Inteligencia Sentiente*: vol. 1, *Inteligencia y realidad*; vol. 2, *Inteligencia y Logos*; vol. 3, *Inteligencia y razon*, cited by Lee, "Liberation Theology's Transcendent Moment," 228 n.13.

97. Zubiri, *El problema teologal del hombre*, 59.

98. Lee, "Liberation Theology's Transcendent Moment," 232.

99. Zubiri, *Nature, History, God*, 333.

100. Zubiri, *Nature, History, God*, 349.

101. Lee, "Liberation Theology's Transcendent Moment," 234.

102. Lee, "Liberation Theology's Transcendent Moment," 234.

Thus, scholars of both Zubiri and Ellacuría do not hesitate to affirm that Ellacuría's work represents the explicitly theological expression of the philosophical-theological elaboration of the human encounter with Zubiri's reality. In a fundamental writing, Ellacuría articulates the theological method based on the tripartite dimension of human "encounter" or "confrontation" with reality.[103]

This "encounter," which is also a "confrontation," Ellacuría describes and elaborates with the Spanish word *cargo* (with its verb forms *cargar* or *encargarse*)—meaning a duty, a weight, or a burden. For Ellacuría, the encounter with real things actually involves and implies:

- *el hacerse cargo de la realidad* (making a commitment to carry reality)

- *el cargar con la realidad* (carrying the weight of reality)

- *el encargarse de la realidad* (taking charge of reality)

Reality for Ellacuría, as for Zubiri, has thickness and weight, and therefore it is necessary to make the commitment to carry it (*hacerse cargo*); to carry the weight on their shoulders (*cargar con*); and to assume as its own the weight of reality (*encargarse*). So reality is something it is necessary to know, something that goes beyond merely objective knowledge to a knowledge that implies the opening of the totality of the person, an effort to know reality as it really is. Theologically, this means looking at historical reality and discovering in it its theological elements and potentials, as in the Vatican Council, *Gaudium et Spes*, which was said to "discern the signs of the times."[104] Here is clearly Zubiri's "theological" conception of conceiving reality as rooted in, or rewired in, God This, for Ellacuría, is what establishes the relation of a concept—be it philosophical or theological—of the historical reality.

One of Ellacuría's greatest contributions was the elaboration of an ethics. And this ethics is an ethics of liberation. As you study it, you see clearly present the anthropological background of Zubiri. Its goal was to elaborate an ethic and a philosophy of history that took off from Zubirian philosophy. He believes that from this, a new way of understanding history can be found. This is why one of his most famous books is titled *Filosofia de la realidad histórica*.[105]

---

103. Ellacuría, *Liberacion y cautiverio*, 626.

104. *Gaudium et Spes*, n. 1.

105. Ellacuría, *Filosofia de la realidad histórica*.

In saying that it is necessary to "charge with reality" (*cargar con*), Ellacuría is elaborating on the ethical correlative of the noetic characteristic of "committing to the charge of reality" (*encargarse de*). The encounter of the human being with reality is situated and dated, has a specific place and time. This offers the human being the opportunity to make genuine and serious commitments by staying within reality and embracing their demands. Therefore, according to Ellacuría, inspired by Zubiri, the knowledge of transcendence does not result from a flight away from historical reality, but in its opposite. It involves a noetic moment that is open to the real and the ethical choice of *locus*, whose combination involves human action.

From this derives the third component of the Ellacurian reading of reality and its philosophical-theological application. To this known and ethically assumed reality, it has to be transformed, to be in charge of transforming it (*encargarse de la realidad*). By taking charge, Ellacuría means the transformation of reality through action or praxis. This praxis transforms reality and correlatively transforms the human being as well. Theologically, conversion and discipleship correspond to the burden of reality, which must be transformed.[106] The dynamics of Ellacuría's reflection, therefore, with its noetic, ethical, and praxic dimensions, do not become a purely materialistic enterprise.[107] On the contrary, following the philosophy of Zubiri, the transcendent God, who cannot be described as something else within reality, nevertheless remains involved with the world as the one who lives and makes things be. This reflection of Ellacuría speaks not only of a creator and sustainer of reality, but of a God who saves reality.[108]

From all this reflection emerges a concept called the "fundamental option." Essential to the development of what will be the option for the poor, assumed by the whole church of the Latin American continent, this concept will place the theme of poverty at the center of the debate and not only affect the social or categorical plan, but not least the transcendental order. And in this sense, the question we are now asking is whether to determine what the church's fundamental choice should be in the face of social reality.

---

106. The use of the term "praxis" brought to Ellacuría accusations of being Marxist and corresponding persecutions. However, his commentators argue that this is ignoring the framework of Ellacuría's work that rests on the assumption of the theological dimension of reality. Lee, "Liberation Theology's Transcendent Moment," 236 n. 43.

107. Jon Sobrino adds to these three moments a fourth moment: letting himself be carried by reality (graceful moment) in the sense of "free"; a "free" moment. Sobrino, "El Ellacuría olvidado," 76 n. 12.

108. Lee, "Liberation Theology's Transcendent Moment."

In Ellacuría's thought, this fundamental option has to be the option for the poor, because the fundamental option is not something the believer adds to the ethical act, which in itself is autonomous. It is the transcendental dimension of the world; that is, a way of seeing things and reality that is very different from the idealistic, whether Hegelian or Marxist. And so, this will put us in front of a new way of understanding history and, consequently, ethics: neither idealist nor materialistic, but realistic.

Aided by Zubiri's philosophy, he attempts to elaborate an ethics of praxis and finds a third way of understanding history, which points in the direction of this perspective, neither Marxist nor idealistic, but realistic. The results of this intuition will appear in the posthumous book we have already quoted here called *Filosofía de la realidad histórica.*[109] For Ellacuría—in the *illumination* of Karl Rahner and other great contemporary theologians—there are not two stories, but one. This is the story of salvation, and it can be equally of perdition.[110]

For Ellacuría, the Christian is called to historicize his faith, to make it take root in history, to make an ethical commitment and to give a *praxical* answer to the demands that history directs on him. Thus, Ellacuría's view of discipleship, of Christian action in the world, cannot be separated from his soteriology. Every story is potentially the history of salvation, instead of story of salvation. Christian praxis—personal or institutional—is called upon to commit itself to make this salvation visible and palpable. His reflection on the encounter with reality in three dimensions—noetic, ethical, and praxic—challenges Christians of yesterday and today, from the north or south, to realize that oppression not only springs from directly oppressive and violent gestures, but also from the quiet and silent decision to compromise with structures that contribute to global oppression.[111] Thus, the president of UCA challenges the confessional university.

In his 1982 speech at the University of Santa Clara, California, Ellacuría very eloquently expressed this conviction in favor of promoting justice in the apostolate of education:

> A Christian university must take into account the preference for
> the gospel of the poor. This does not mean that the poorest must

109. Ellacuría, *Filosofía de la realidad historica.*

110. Rahner, *Curso Fundamental da fé* (English versión: *Foundations of Christian Faith: An Introduction to the Idea of Christianity*).

111. Rahner, *Curso Fundamental da fé* (English versión: *Foundations of Christian Faith: An Introduction to the Idea of Christianity*).

be those who enter to study at the university, nor that the university should give up cultivating the academic excellence necessary to solve the real problems that affect its social context. It does mean that the university must incarnate among the poor intellectually in order to be science for those without a voice, intellectual support for those who in the same reality have truth and reason, albeit sometimes as spoliation, but they have no academic reasons to justify and legitimize their truth and reason.[112]

The mission that Ellacuría had in his hands after 1979 was to govern a university. There he tries to make the best of a happy synthesis of what he thinks with his philosophy and his theology and what he believes with his faith and experiences with his spirituality: placing the acquired intellectual formation in an institution of the Society of Jesus in charge of studies and intellectual contents serving the poor of his country, El Salvador.

Ignacio Ellacuría: A "Mystical Thought"

Ignacio Ellacuría had at the most profound depth of his intellectual brilliance and his keen prophetic vision and transformative strategy a mystical spirituality. His thought uses spiritual, philosophical, ecclesiological, and theological sources to develop a fundamental contextual theology for Latin America. Together with his community and especially Jon Sobrino, his companion and great interlocutor, he experienced a mystical encounter with the risen Jesus mediated through his love and solidarity with the suffering people of El Salvador. In this he and his community closely followed the Ignatian spirituality that was his own. For Ignatius of Loyola, God is the God of the world, and the world is the place to meet Him.[113]

Therefore, the community who drank of this spirituality will ceaselessly adhere to and connect with the reality of the social, economic, and political context of the country where it is inserted and planted. Do not look at it as something accidental or contingent, but as "locus theologicus." Jon Sobrino himself narrates and describes the UCA project in which he participated with Ellacuría with these words: "we have done

112. Ellacuría, "Commencement Address."

113. St. Ignatius of Loyola, *Spiritual Exercises*, n. 230–38, contemplation to attain love.

nothing more than—beginning with Jesus—to raise the reality we are living to the level of a theological concept."[114]

Ellacuría was Basque by birth, but Salvadoran of nationality and heart. He was a bridge figure, in fact. Robert Lassalle-Klein says Ellacuría "was among the brightest of a generation of mid-twentieth-century Spanish Jesuits sent to serve the Catholic Church of Latin America. But he is loved and remembered above all for having embraced and been transformed by sharing a lifetime of the sufferings, hopes, and aspirations of the 'crucified people' of El Salvador."[115] It is Ellacuría himself then who writes: "It is not we who have to save the poor, but the poor who will save us."[116] Jon Sobrino thus interprets his companion: "the foundation of his life, his vocation as a Jesuit, and even more deeply, as a human being, was to descend the crucified people from the cross."[117]

The reality of an option for the poor, in defense of their dignity and liberation of the exploiters, in Ellacuría, is definitely the fruit, on the one hand, of the spirituality of the exercises of St. Ignatius, deeply rooted within; and on the other, the example of his archbishop and friend Oscar Arnulfo Romero. It is also the result of his Christian faith and the experience of a lifetime deepening and cultivating a spirituality: Ignatian spirituality. It was prepared throughout life by the action-oriented mysticism of the *Spiritual Exercises of St. Ignatius*, led by his novice master Miguel Elizondo and strengthened by fellows who shared the same sense of call to mission in the Society of Jesus in Latin America.[118] From this emerges a whole dimension of the president of UCA and his entire community that may risk being forgotten or at least in the shadow.

Father Juan Hernandez-Pico, Jesuit of the Central American Province, will say about Ellacuría: "What Ignacio Ellacuría did in his apostolic life as a mature Jesuit, although he did not programmatically formulate it in these words, was primarily to lead the Province from Central America to enter the spirit of the *Spiritual Exercises* . . . and later the . . . UCA. So finally, building on that, he tried to bring the national reality of El Salvador through the same experience."[119]

114. Nephew, *Jesucristo liberador*, 30.

115. Lassalle-Klein, *Blood and Ink*, 190.

116. Ellacuría, "El tercer mundo," 127–38.

117. Sobrino, *Ignacio Ellacuría*, 5.

118. Lassalle-Klein, *Blood and Ink*, 188.

119. Sobrino and Alvarado, *Ignatio Ellacuría*, 305.

Matthew Ashley, author of an important study on the influence of the *Spiritual Exercises* on Ignacio Ellacuría, states: "The briefest look in his biography makes it clear that Ignacio Ellacuría was a man passionately committed to Ignatian spirituality, who sought to put it at the service of church in Latin America. . . . He did this largely by seeking philosophical and theological language and arguments to articulate the encounter with Christ, which is structured by Ignatius Loyola's *Spiritual Exercises*."[120]

One perspective from which one can better understand the influence of Ignatian spirituality on Ellacuría is the tension that is so present between the universal and particular. This is what lies at the heart of Ignatian spirituality: "not being restrained to the fullest, but fitting in the minimum, is a divine thing."[121] This phrase is dedicated to St. Ignatius in a symbolic epitaph included in a nearly 1,000-page work, the *Imago primi sæculi Societatis Iesu*, which the Society of Jesus edited to celebrate its first centenary in 1640. It can be translated thus: "It is divine not to be limited by the largest and yet be contained in the smallest."[122]

Saint Ignatius was always a man of great desires, who had high aspirations and dreamed high. However, he was convinced—because God himself had taught him—that the greatest and the smallest must walk together, complement each other, and refer to each other. Therefore, in his *Spiritual Exercises*, the exerciser is invited to discover the presence of God in the greatest and the least imaginable. God is beyond all the remotest, poorest, and furthest places the Society of Jesus could have come to; and also from the great scholars, cultures, ideologies, or sciences that the Jesuits found and worked with; and also beyond your wildest wishes. For these great desires, if not embodied in the "limited," the small, or a concrete social and ecclesial insertion, are illusory and not real.[123]

Understanding this well means taking care of the small, one's own smallness and others, their own and others' suffering. It is supposed to deal with the injustice that is felt as a blow, having the greatness to fight it to win it and overcome it. Wanting to end world poverty, and not fight the same poverty that reduces and eliminates lives where one lives and works, is to cheat yourself and others. The *Spiritual Exercises*[124] are so universal, as seen

---

120. Ashley, "Contemplation in the Action of Justice," 144.

121. "Ejercicios espirituales."

122. Bingemer, *Em tudo amar e servir*, 213.

123. Bingemer, *Em tudo amar e servir*, 213.

124. St. Ignatius of Loyola, *Spiritual Exercises*, nn. 91–98.

in contemplation of the kingdom, and the goal they propose passes through the minimum, the offering of life by following Jesus Christ in poverty, humiliation, insults, and contempt in the world.[125]

What Ignatius had in mind was an apostolic community sent on a mission to preach the Gospel to every creature and every nation in the name of the Father, the Son, and the Holy Spirit. This universal vision is reinforced by the contemplation of the Incarnation of Exercises[126] where the three divine persons—Father, Son, and Holy Spirit—look lovingly upon the surface of the earth and see all mankind. And what they see is a divided humanity. Divided by different races (some white, some black); by violence (some in peace and others in war); by happiness and sadness (some crying, others laughing); by health and physical condition (some healthy, some sick); by the moment of life where they are (some being born and some dying).[127]

The Trinity's "decision" to send the Son to redeem humanity is made by looking at this whole world with all these divisions that reflect injustice and violence and nonacceptance of differences. And the implementation of this decision can be contemplated in the poor house of a poor young woman, anonymous and of no importance on the social scale, on the last periphery of the time and space where she lives: Mary of Nazareth, pregnant by the Holy Spirit.[128]

This means that the universality expressed in kingdom meditation implies a preference and a particularity. God wants to save the whole world, but starting from the bottom. He looks at creation and sees where the problems lie and where justice and peace are lacking and the people are suffering. His preference is for those who are in distress and in need and there the incarnate Word shall be born, grow, and assume his public ministry. The poor and humble Christ of St. Ignatius' *Spiritual Exercises* devoted himself wholly to helping the poor, healing the sick, feeding the hungry, giving sight to the blind, and making the lame walk. These are the signs of the kingdom that the Gospel puts in Jesus' mouth in response to

---

125. Cf. n. 98 of St. Ignatius of Loyola, *Spiritual Exercises*: "Eternal Lord of all things, I offer my oblation with your favor and help . . . protesting that I want and desire, by deliberate determination, to imitate you to endure all insult, all ignominy and all poverty, both material and spiritual . . . as long as this is for your greatest service and praise."

126. St. Ignatius of Loyola, *Spiritual Exercises*, nn. 101–9.

127. St. Ignatius of Loyola, *Spiritual Exercises*, n. 106.

128. St. Ignatius of Loyola, *Spiritual Exercises*, nn. 101–10, contemplation of the Incarnation

the Baptist's emissaries who approach it to ask themselves and the Messiah.[129] If the signs of the kingdom happen, and if this configures the coming of the Messiah, then yes, God's kingdom is already in the midst of all. But if injustice reigns, if there are still people suffering, then there is enough to say that the kingdom of God has come.

Ignatius felt and understood very deeply this dramatic tension between universality and particularity. In this way, he proposes that the one who does the Exercises go into poverty to preach poverty and to be received under the banner of Jesus Christ, in great spiritual and present poverty, in a life of humiliation and humility. After feeling and experiencing this revelation from God and having founded the Society of Jesus, Ignatius makes each candidate go beyond the experience of the Exercises through experiments of service to the poor, to the sick; living alms on pilgrimage in the poorest conditions, etc. It is very clear from the founder's desire that his followers could live near the poor to feel and share their situation and make others share this compassion to help them.

The Jesuits practiced many ministries, some very important. With kings and emperors, with intellectuals of the highest level. They were founders of important educational establishments. But they have always been mindful of the poor and oppressed of society in their time and sent their missionaries to the poorest parts of the world: Latin America, Africa, and Asia. We must admit that in this they followed the colonial movement of that time, when Europe was "discovering" different parts of the world and the colonizers arrived with the sword and the cross. Christian colonization certainly cannot boast that it has greatly respected the differences of colonized peoples, especially as regards their religious beliefs and their cultural matrices.

Other religious orders did this too (Franciscans, Dominicans, etc.). But the Jesuits had a different way of proceeding. First of all regarding inculturation. They were the only modern religious order that understood the inseparability between evangelization of inculturation. About entering and assuming the culture of the other, the Society of Jesus has a glorious tradition, in which Guarani's reductions shine in South America, Matteo Ricci's experiences with Roberto Nobili's Malabar rites, and so many others. Its educational system has been "globalized" from the outset because of its presence in these distant and poor parts of the world.[130] Their efforts were

129. Matt 11:5.

130. Cf. for example, St. Francis Xavier asking the company to send Jesuits to Japan, etc.

to educate the poor just as they did the rich and to turn their institutions and jobs to those who were oppressed and unimportant on the social scale. This has reduced inequalities at least culturally. In this, their efforts were globalized, but they could not reach their goals because of the many difficulties they themselves encountered in their path.[131]

It is legitimate to hope that today, with a more accurate awareness of the phenomenon of globalization and with so many other resources, Ignatius' inspired and wise vision and understanding of evangelizing work can produce good results, especially in the regions of the globe that need them most.

Ellacuría and his community lived this spirituality. Jon Sobrino, Ellacuría's companion and friend, deals with this theme in his article "El Ellacuría Olvidado. Lo que no se puede dilapidar."[132] The author maintains in this article:

> The reasons why these themes are forgotten seem to me as follows. The main one is that we do not seriously commit ourselves to "the crucified people," and they question us and can also accuse us: Yes, what do we have to do with the crucifixion of peoples? The "civilization of poverty" and its salvific potentiality unsettle us, because it is something that challenges reason and rationality and then provokes scandal. And the God who is present in the martyrs and victims—the greater and at the same time lesser God—can understandably leave the non-believer indifferent, though not necessarily so, because in his experience the question of how he is dynamically present can emerge—if at all, makes the ultimate positivity of the story. And for what he believes this is mandatory in order to question what God he believes in and what God he does not believe, without being able to defend himself with anything, nor doctrines or liturgies, from the radicality of the matter.[133]

131. We can mention here the many setbacks encountered by the Society of Jesus in Portugal and also in Latin America with the decree of Pombal that extinguished it, the expulsion of the Jesuits from so many countries, the annihilation of the experience of the Guarani republic, etc.

132. Sobrino, "El Ellacuría olvidado," 69–96.

133. Sobrino, "El Ellacuría olvidado," 70 (translation ours). In the original Spanish: "Las razones por las que se olvidan estos temas me parecen ser las siguientes. La principal es que introducirnos en serio en 'el pueblo crucificado' nos cuestiona e incluso puede llegar a acusarnos: sí y qué tenemos que ver nosotros, como personas e intelectuales, con la crucifixión de los pueblos. 'La civilización de la pobreza' y su potencial salvífico nos desinstala, pues para la razón tiene mucho de locura y escándalo. Y 'el Dios que se

Jon Sobrino, in this excellent article, recalls three points of the mysticism that Ellacuría lived, transmitted, reflected, and left as legacy, which are inseparable from his thinking as a whole.[134] They are: firstly the question of the crucified people who must be brought down from the cross, knowing that in doing so one can end up on the cross in trying. Secondly, the challenge of working for a civilization of poverty, contrary to and surpassing the civilization of wealth, responsible for the grave illness of the prevailing civilization. Thirdly, his words "with Monsignor Romero, God passed through El Salvador," which more generally refers to something ultimate and beneficial, which is present in the history of the victims' defenders.[135]

Jon Sobrino continues to draw attention to the fact that in these three points appears the principle of partiality of God, confirming the dialectical tension so present in the Exercises of St. Ignatius and so dear to Ellacuría between universal and particular. The revelation of God appears as partial, which forces us to overcome an abstract universalism not in any way, but from the "underground" of history,[136] that is from the reality of the poor and the victims. This reality, according to the author, is the bearer of truth and salvation. And also, in Christian terms, of the flesh of God, both humiliated and full of salvation. And there is also the demand for a praxis—another central term in Ellacuría's thought—but not any praxis, instead one that is liberation to the oppressed.[137]

With this emphasis given to these points of inseparability between thought and mysticism—or we could even say of Ellacuría's "mystical thought"—one is free from the risk of forgetting the main of his contribution, emphasizes Jon Sobrino. Moreover, it takes seriously enough what the author calls "the total Ellacuría." In this total Ellacuría, Jon Sobrino draws attention to and presents, beyond the undeniable influence of Zubiri, Ranher,

hace presente en mártires y víctimas'—Dios mayor y simultáneamente menor—al no creyente comprensiblemente le puede dejar indiferente, aunque no necesariamente, pues en su experiencia puede asomar la pregunta de a través de qué se hace dinámicamente presente—si es que lo hay—lo último positivo de la historia. Y al creyente le exige preguntarse en qué Dios cree y en qué Dios no cree, sin poderse defender con nada, ni con doctrinas y liturgias, de la radicalidad de la pregunta."

134. Sobrino, "El Ellacuría olvidado," 69–96.

135. Sobrino, "El Ellacuría olvidado," 70.

136. Because it is difficult to translate Spanish "abajo" as used by the theologian, I chose here to translate something literal and may seem strange in English, but not in theology.

137. Sobrino, "El Ellacuría olvidado," 70.

and Marx, a core of themes that remain more in the shadow: that is, the mystic Ellacuría, his spirituality, and what gave sense to his life.

Jon Sobrino then explicitly mentions there among these religious traditions: "the biblical-Jesuit tradition, that of Saint Ignatius of Loyola, that of Monsignor Romero," and he adds, "These traditions, in addition to their potential for shaping life, also have the potential for shaping thought. The intellectual Ellacuría is not fully known without capturing his understanding of the Exercises of St. Ignatius, the homilies of Monsignor Romero and, of course, of the reported and reflected reality of Jesus of Nazareth. And to this must be added the impact that Salvadoran reality had on his thinking . . . and what these realities gave him to think about, and also what helped him to think and conceptualize reality."[138]

Jon Sobrino's argument will reach its focal point when he mentions a third reason why it seems to him that these themes are often overlooked when talking about Ellacuría. This third reason is not to put in relation to the martyrial death of Ellacuría and his thought. That is, as if martyrdom had to do with the religious or political Ellacuría and not with the intellectual Ellacuría. As the author rightly says, "I do not know whether an intellectual's way of dying easily becomes too—once dead—a principle of understanding the fundamentals of his thinking."[139] The theologian thinks—and we agree—that Ellacuría's way of dying and his tension and approaching this death in life help to deepen what he meant by the two evoked and sometimes forgotten concepts: "crucified people" and "civilization." The closeness to poverty and to Monsignor Romero was, for Ellacuría and for many in El Salvador, the incarnate presence of God. As with Jesus of Nazareth, death illuminates life and thought, and it is meaningless and cannot be read and interpreted without this life and this thought.

The seal of martyrial death seals life and thought and gives it a special light that does not allow them to take their weight and depth and easily forget them. There is no means to forget why Ellacuría lived, thought, and died, and this is the reason to lead a project and a community that would be an unforgettable witness to the whole world. Martyrdom gives an invaluable seal to all this. And even more—we add—Ellacuría did not live it alone, but in community. Community that was his, there at the university, but which extended beyond the borders of El Salvador, because this community comprised and embraced the entire apostolic body of the Society

138. Sobrino, "El Ellacuría olvidado," 70–71.

139. Sobrino, "El Ellacuría olvidado," 71.

of Jesus, the whole church of the poor that emerged in Latin America after the council, and the whole universal church in her sincere effort to tirelessly serve the project of the kingdom of God.

The superior general of the Society, Father Kolvenbach, had reaffirmed this evangelical and pastoral choice, which was Ellacuría's and so many others, when, on March 8, 1988, before the Jesuit community massacre, he declared to the students at Mass, during the beginning of classes at the UCA of San Salvador:

> You know that as Jesuits we were challenged and questioned by the Gospel of the Lord, by the social documents of the Church and by the cries of the poor of this earth who ascend to heaven. This is why we reformulate our mission today: faith and the defense of faith means the effort to keep alive the Gospel of the Lord Jesus and faith in the kingdom of God among us; and it is the promotion of justice, that is, the transformation of a world of oppression and sin into a world of life and brotherhood. We also saw that we should do this in the preferential option for the poor, looking at God and the world at large from their point of view, letting us inspire for them and placing ourselves at their service in the joint effort of all and divine grace. I believe this university has made a serious effort to fulfill this Christian and human ideal here in El Salvador. This is what leads it to tell the truth about the country, to analyze its structures, to denounce oppression and to propose just and viable solutions. This is what leads her to speak of God and the Gospel as good news for everyone, particularly the poor. This is what now and concretely drives her to work for a just peace and to maintain the hope of the poor.[140]

Living and Dying in Community

It cannot be said that the murder of the entire Jesuit community took the Jesuits completely by surprise. The priests knew it was dangerous to be there. Many had warned them. But they were committed to those people they had learned to love. What followed was the murder of Father Rutilio Grande, Monsignor Romero, and the three sisters—Maura Clarke, Ita Ford, Dorothy Kazel, and laywoman Jean Donovan—who had been living and mourning, their hearts bleeding following the ongoing murder of hundreds

---

140. Kolvenbach, "El Salvador." Visit of the Jesuit General Superior.

of peasants and catechists, poor men and women, and even children and old people who were killed with barbaric violence.

They had read on the walls of San Salvador the terrible and bloody phrase: "Haga patria, mate un cura!" (Be patriotic, kill a priest). But they chose to stay, to stand by the side of the people they were serving. Their theology, the spirituality that inspired them, told them that leaving could not be the solution. They owed their lives to those people who had no right to life and who had been decimated by injustice and the terror of violence.

Their form of contribution to the people was the teachings of the university that they carried forward. Their commitment, therefore, was academic and pastoral. It would also become martyrial. Robert Lassalle-Klein expresses it beautifully in his book *Blood and Ink*.[141] The author, in the introduction, raises the question: "Why involve virtually the entire command structure of the Salvadoran army and possibly the president in order to kill a priest and a handful of his collaborators?"[142] He concludes his introduction by stating:

> This is a story of blood and ink; of writers, books, teaching, service projects, and learning dedicated to revealing the truth about the state-sponsored, US-tax-financed persecution of civil society. But above all is the story of a university's efforts to help bring down the crucified people of El Salvador from their cross, supporting their efforts to build a society in which everyone had a chance to share a future where dignity, love, compassion and health could prevail.[143]

At the Monsignor Romero Center, in the UCA, the memories of Romero and those of Rutilio Grande are gathered, deaths that marked the beginning of the conversion of the Archbishop and the Jesuits murdered in November 1989. One museum exhibit, a book stained with blood, draws the attention and makes the visitor tremble. It is no coincidence that it is entitled *El Dios Crucificado* and is authored by the great Reformed German theologian Jürgen Moltmann.

When the military who perpetrated the murder of Ignacio Ellacuría and his other comrades dragged the corpse of Juan Ramon Moreno into the room of Jon Sobrino (the only member of the community who was outside at that time and was therefore saved from the killing), the book fell from the shelf over Moreno's bloody body. This is how it is preserved

141. Lassalle-Klein, *Blood and Ink*.

142. Lassalle-Klein, *Blood and Ink*, 20.

143. Lassalle-Klein, *Blood and Ink*, 23.

in the museum to this day. It would be a delicate way that God chose to show Jon Sobrino's presence alongside his martyred community, even though he was far away. He, with his theology, would be responsible for not letting his memory die and all that his fellow martyrs fought for. The book stained with the blood of Juan Ramon Moreno is the tangible testimony of Sobrino's unbroken solidarity with his community.

The military had come the day before the massacre. They had come in, reviewed everything, and after that they left without finding any subversive material. That night the community thought they would be safe, that no one would molest them. They did not realize that this was simply "ground reconnaissance" so that they could better plan the fatal attack.

The two women who were killed along with the Jesuits were mother and daughter. They were the wife and daughter of the gardener Obdulio Ramos, who took care of the house and garden of the Jesuit residence and who, after the death of the Jesuits and his wife and daughter, planted the rose garden that still adorns the tombs of the dead.

Julia Elba Ramos and Celina Maristela Ramos were killed because the military did not want witnesses to what they had done. The Jesuits were all killed together, in a circle, lying on the floor face down. The next morning, Mr. Obdulio met them and the Jesuits. He immediately called the provincial, Father Tojeira, SJ, to report what had happened.

A witness, a woman named Lucia, told what she heard and saw from the window of the neighboring house where she lived. She told her story over and over, but had to leave the country for security reasons.

The Meaning and Legacy of the Martyrdom of the UCA Community

In fact, the martyrdom and legacy of this pioneering and visionary community of UCA lies in the very model of university it wanted to build. Under Ellacuría's direction, UCA turned from a developmental rhetoric corresponding to its inauguration in 1965[144] to an institution whose mission was to serve the oppressed nation where it was situated with creative and critical awareness. Ignacio Ellacuría was always seeing this more clearly as he committed himself to this work, whether as a teacher, trainer, or dean.[145]

144. Beirne, *Jesuit Education*, 227.

145. Cf. Ellacuría, "Is a Different Kind of University Possible"; and Ellacuría, "Las Funciones Fundamentales."

The horizon of this university was the Salvadoran people. It was, therefore an ex-centric, outward-looking university immersed in the national reality of an unjust society in constant exodus toward the poor who should benefit from the knowledge produced there. The cultured "word" of the university was nonetheless scholarly, but it wanted and had to be effective in its Christian inspiration, its academic programs, and the major concrete problems facing the nation, such as land reform, education, economic justice, and an end to the causes of the civil war that was destroying the country and its people.[146]

It is worth mentioning Charles J. Beirne in his excellent book, *Jesuit Education and Social Change in El Salvador*: "UCA was determined not to stay on the banks, sending occasional good wishes to those who were fighting; UCA put itself on the side of the poor and tried to be their voice until the day they could speak for themselves. It took sides, but in the way that Ignacio Ellacuría constantly insisted—as a university (universiariamente)."[147]

In addition to the university spirit, the community spirit was fundamental in UCA. It has always been a community who ruled it, not individuals who do not add their strength with others or consult with each other. The traditional "body spirit" of the Society of Jesus can be clearly understood by contemplating the "UCA case."[148] From the beginning, this apostolic community thought together, prayed together, and acted together, with one goal on the horizon, and this was already being gestated in the minds of their superiors. The superiors were sent to study abroad and several of them—among others, Ellacuría, Jon Sobrino, and Amando Lopez—were to return to take up their positions in the UCA and other works of the province, always aiming at this social transformation.

When they returned, they helped transform the Society of Jesus itself and its institutions—including UCA—into a new focus on the preferential option for the poor. The former dean, Luis Achaerandio, always supported them in this way, as well as the provincial superiors such as Miguel Francisco Estrada and Cesar Jerez, the latter having sent several to study abroad to later compose the community of UCA—Ignacio Martín Baró, Segundo Montes, and Rodolfo Cardenal. In addition, they always

146. Beirne, *Jesuit Education*, 228.

147. Beirne, *Jesuit Education*, 228.

148. Cf. Bertrand, *Un corps pour l'Esprit*; Bertrand, "A corps pour Esprit"; and Desroche, *Évolution de l'Image*, 202–3.

had the encouragement of superiors in Rome, such as Pedro Arrupe and Peter Hans Kolvenbach.

Some worked together on the same ministry. Or in other similar works (such as UCA and CIAS).[149] But all were friends with one another and shared the same ideals and expressed this sharing by supporting or confronting fellow members in matters concerning the action of the community and the work. They experienced together misunderstandings and persecutions; they were often questioned; they always sought to link their theoretical vision with concrete projects and then evaluate the results. At the same time they taught, administered, wrote, spoke, and made public statements. In the meantime, they took care of each other to continue living under the barrage of conflicts, oppositions, and threats they had to endure.[150]

They shared risks of all kinds, including life, and gave courage to each other in hard times. Sometimes they argued strongly with each other about the new vision of the university they wanted to implement. And they all gathered to mourn their first martyr, Rutilio Grande, in 1977. Occasionally some had to go into exile, especially in the 1970s.[151] But they never stopped working together, especially thinking ahead, writing seminal documents, and devising processes to implement them.

Their mysticism as a community was one of their main legacies and testimonies. And those who killed them knew it. They were not only murdering Ellacuría, but an entire community. The group was shot in the head (literally),[152] but they wanted to kill the whole group. The presence of the two women who belonged to the people the Jesuits served with all their passion and ability is strongly symbolic in their martyrdom.[153] The poor had become a constituent part of that university community and were present even in the martyrdom that sealed their testimony.

No one yet knows the details of either the killing or the dialogue between the murderers and the Jesuits. But everyone knows that they died because of what they were and did, because of what they lived, and because they refused to leave or abandon the people they served. From

149. Center for Research and Social Action (CIAS) were centers that researched the social reality in multidisciplinary terms. Several were created in all the provinces of the company, after the 32nd General Congregation of the Society of Jesus.

150. Beirne, *Jesuit Education*, 230.

151. "Martires de la UCA."

152. I have seen the pictures taken from the Jesuits' corpses and witnessed this terrible cruelty.

153. Cf. Jon Sobrino mentions Julia Elba and Celina as "very dear daughters of God."

the outset it was clear that this was not a case of an isolated person, but of an entire community. The killers were not only aimed at the dean, though perhaps mainly at him. The whole community died believing that another world is possible and fighting for it.

In the discussions that followed the community's assassination, it is critical to recall that the martyrs had expressed their fear that there would be no more Jesuits available to succeed them in the near future and that the UCA might have to entrust laypeople with decision-making positions. And while it is desirable that this should happen not only at UCA, but at all the universities of the Society of Jesus—a greater participation of lay companions of mysticism and spirit—one cannot forget the whole movement made by the Society of Jesus to fill the void left by the martyrdom of the companions.[154]

The Central American Jesuits and the superior general at the time, Father Peter Hans Kolvenbach, invited a good number of Jesuits to replace the martyrs[155] and the community has gathered itself and continues to work there today to the same extent and with the same enthusiasm, faithful to the memory and legacy of the martyrs.

Some feared that UCA had been expropriated from their soul with the murdered community. This is explainable because each martyr held various positions within the university—vice deans, department directors, professors, and so on—but it didn't happen. The successors tried to rebuild the university from within rather than completely mimic what the martyrs did. UCA continued with its tradition of being present and publicly speaking on relevant national issues, as the need after the Jesuits' death was even greater than before.[156]

The testimony the martyrs leave is that one can kill the body but not the spirit. And the spirit of the murdered community continued and lives on in the Jesuits who later occupied their posts and carried on the university, as well as in the laypeople who share this mission with them.

The mysticism that presided over UCA has always been communal. The creation and development of his model was communitarian, communal persecution he suffered, communal witness, and martyrdom. As

---

154. Among the Jesuits who offered themselves to go to the UCA after the massacre of the community are theologians from all over the world such as German Martin Maier, SJ, or American Dean Brackley, SJ, recently deceased, among others.

155. Beirne, *Jesuit Education*, 221–22.

156. Beirne, *Jesuit Education*, 221–22.

the beautiful posthumous prayer that Jesuit Ricardo Falla, SJ, wrote to Ellacuría says:

Prayer to Ignacio Ellacuría[157]

Assassinated in San Salvador on November 16, 1989

Ellacu, they destroyed your head with bullets. Your gray head stood on the grass. She ran out of thoughts, like a room without light. Your enemies hated you and wanted to destroy your great intelligence. They considered you the brain of subversion within the UCA and the Church. They do not know that your ideas are intact and are working in thousands of hearts within El Salvador and around the world.

Ellacu, the word was silenced. They gagged you with the damp earth of dawn. Many times they have listened to you from the National Reality Chair at UCA and on television news. Your word was sharp and merciless against injustice. Your word unveiled the masks of the most subtle mistakes. Now, from the highest elevation of the university building, as on Mount Calvary, you will continue to speak more forcefully. Perhaps you will now achieve what you could not in life, the conversion of your enemies. Forgive them because they really don't know what they are doing.

Ellacu, they left you lying face down. Are you desperate? Don't you wanna look at the November stars anymore? Utopian ages indeed. You thought of a third gallows, you wanted to negotiate, you tried too hard to be a mediator, you sought peace in this storm of hatred, from the University you wanted to open a different path and you listened to politicians of all parties, scanned ambassadors, lent the chair to academics, meeting distant commitments. You were really Utopian, but a Utopian who never crossed his arms. See you now with your face to the ground. Did you despair? Did you throw the towel? We began to understand that the third gallows were not outsourcing, that negotiation was not lameness, that criticism of revolutionaries was no obstacle to liberation, that your conversations with the president were not betrayal of the poor. Now your utopia, now that you have failed to realize it, begins to light our way.

157. The Prayer to Ignacio Ellacuría is provided in full from Falla, "Oración a Ignacio Ellacuría."

Ellacu, they left you lying forever with your brothers. You were their leader. You dragged them to death. There you have yours, always faithful. Then you have them, docile, following you to the end, willing to let you down even if sometimes you were very demanding with them. You didn't die alone. You died in community. The enemies were not mistaken. You were not alone. You were with yours. Without them you were nobody.

Ellacu, they stole your Comin Prize. They took you out of your room while others killed you. Where are those 5,000 dollars? Your master was sold for 30 coins. They paid more for you and the workers on Opico's farm ran out of houses. Your enemies stole your prize. Do not worry. You have friends. Remember your travels to the Netherlands, the United States, Spain. . . . UCA's farm workers will not be helpless.

Ellacu, did they touch your heart? You have bullets in the back. Did someone scrape your heart? It was hard to reach your heart. Sometimes you seemed just head, you just seemed justice without mercy. But in your own way you were tender, you were loving, you needed to express yourself. You needed children. You madly wanted offspring. You were carrying a void and a shadow accompanied you.

Ellacu, why did you let yourself be killed? So smart and you didn't guess Monday's attack was ground reconnaissance. Your analysis was potent, but you had no feeling. You trusted the reason. You did not know the time of darkness. Twice you came out in other years from El Salvador, as your Master when you crossed the Jordan. Now you have come too euphoric from Europe, full of plans and projects. You have fallen into the trap that you have been setting for a long time. Or maybe you were ready to accept your time and seal your word with blood.

Ellacu, weren't you afraid at the last minute? Didn't you feel the rush of adrenaline when midnight bombs smashed the window panes? You were tremendously serene! You still got your robe on. You still put on some sandals so you don't hurt your feet. You wanted to face the captain of the operation as a truly magnificent dean.

Ellacu, did you pray before you died? We see you saying mass, university priest. But it's hard for us to imagine asking for help. Your final posture, however, is that of Jesus in the garden with his face to the ground as a sign of downcast worship. Ellacu, remember now that you are in the kingdom. Speak to the Father, use your dialectic, do not invent sophistry. These are no longer worth it. Tell Him to hear the cries of this people. Your best point now and your blood.

Before, some did not believe you very much. We said you spoke from the UCA air conditioner. Now you have become dirty, you have annihilated yourself as your master, you have emptied your strength and the remnants of your pride in the same land of all. Your Father will at this time hear your priestly prayer.

The martyr community is still alive in the tireless efforts of those working at the university, of the many students who come to it not only from El Salvador, but from all over the world, to drink from the spirit and legacy there. More than thirty years later, the UCA community continues to inspire individuals, communities, and universities to follow Jesus and build His kingdom.

Conclusion: Martyrdom as
a Community Liturgy

AT THE END OF these reflections, we ask ourselves: what message do these two communities leave us today?

First, they were both revolutionary, each in its own style. But their ways of transformatively marking the world was certainly no less countercultural, each according to its charisma and style of spirituality. They lived in a way that was different from the usual model of religious community.

Second, they brought something new about how to live consecration to God and others. Both were dealing with news brought by the Second Vatican Council and assumed by the whole church, but were just beginning to be assimilated and practiced. Tibhirine demonstrated the commitment to the end, to the blood, with interreligious dialogue. They lived in a country where the religion of the other was majority and practiced the monastic life that was theirs in close dialogue and in deep communion with this "other" tradition, assuming and integrating various elements. The Jesuits from UCA did the same with the option for the poor. When they died, it was already taken over by the church of Latin America, but they found a way to live it in community and academia. An entire university returned to this option by answering questions that arose about how to live this option while not being poor. Therefore, both communities were pioneers of the choices the Church was beginning to live and were the light that illuminates the path for the others behind.

Third, both communities were embedded in a particular and concrete reality, but with universal openness. Its realities were in Algeria and by extension the Middle East; and in El Salvador, which was now a strategic and explosive point in Central America. But this was a window to the world. In

Algeria and El Salvador they lived the Christian faith as proposed by the gospel of Jesus to every man and woman living in this world.

Fourth, both communities have taken up the challenge of staying despite danger and threat. They did not retreat or escape or make any change in their attitude or position out of fear of taking over themselves and bearing the consequences of their choices. And they were guided by the desire and hope that this would be of universal repercussion.

Fifth, both communities were sustained by a deep spirituality. The whole process they lived until their death was prayed, discerned, worked in community, both "ad intra" and "ad extra," within diversity.

Sixth, both communities had a remarkable leader in front of them. Both Christian de Chergé and Ignacio Ellacuría were anything but charismatic and delusional, unaware of the facts and dangers they faced. Besides being great spirituals, they were also both brilliant intellectuals, with a broad and prophetic vision, who followed the inspirations given to them by God and engaged in projects that their time demanded. Their charisma was fundamental for the communities to engage so deeply in these projects and they responded to the call of the times and the context in which they were located.

Seventh, both communities wanted to bring peace in the midst of conflict, injustice, and violence. Their testimony is evangelical and peaceful, even if violence seems to have had the last word. The future has shown that their gestures, their words, their lives, and their testimonies remain and are victorious over violence.

Eighth, both communities leave us some points of their witness that can be lived by every person, every Christian, in any context, while not needing to be religious, a monk, or anything like that.

Be praying among others, not only Christians, but those of other faiths and religions. Find spiritual nourishment in the other's religion, contributing from your own and learning from the other as well.

Live simply among the poor and at their service. Receive friendship, forgiveness, and the priorities that guide work, even research, academic, and university work.

Do not react to violence with violence. Practice to the extreme the evangelical principle of not returning evil with evil, but reacting to evil with good, love, and peace. In the Tibhirine community this is evident and even made explicit repeatedly by the writings of Christian de Chergé and Christophe Lebreton. In the Salvadoran community, this objective is not clearly stated, but it is practiced to the extent that the Jesuits try in every way to dialogue with various governments and do not close themselves off or refuse to do so. They were killed in dialogue until the end, and not even recognizing the ground of the visit of a group of military personnel the day before the murder of the entire community was a reason for them to flee or take any more explicit defensive measures.

While facing death with a certain style, the style of Jesus Christ; remaining resilient under threat; praying and discerning the possibility of martyrdom; making decisions to stay; and staying true to the commitment to death as a very near horizon, the martyr receives martyrdom as a gift. Violent death through faithfulness to Jesus Christ and his gospel can be accepted but not sought. This is the difference with others who accept both dying and killing. This is not the death of the kamikaze, nor suicide, neither the action of the bomb man, nor the death of Socrates quietly drinking his poison in front of his disciples while uttering wise words. All of them, in some way, bring about death and walk toward it. The martyr, in return, receives it passively. The only thing he does is not get out of his way and not lose clarity about the history given to him to live from the perspective of his faith. This, too, is like Jesus of Nazareth.

Both communities respond, inspired by the Spirit of God, to the challenges that the history of their time faces. They are, as the Second Vatican Council wants, attentive readers of the "signs of the times" that reveal where God's will passes in this time and space. At the same time, their lives and their martyrdom bear witness to the presence and revelation of God, which paradoxically allow themselves to be seen in the powerlessness and failure of the cross, a historical event that configures nascent Christianity—a man who was born, lived, suffered, and died violently in a certain period of human history.[1]

Reading and meditating on the testimony of these two Christian religious communities, we further see that suffering and death are no frontier for God. The early Christian community understood this because when they experienced the resurrection of Jesus, they listened to what God said through his death. From there, they reread the story and realized that they were facing an event not merely linear and chronological, but rather something that turned the story itself on its hinges. A new era was beginning, in which it was necessary to announce the good news and to build the kingdom so that Jesus' proposal could spread throughout the world and not

---

1. Bingemer, "La fe," 175–94; Bingemer, *Dom Oscar Romero.*

be stifled by unsuitable institutions. Christianity is therefore based on the announcement of the kingdom of God made by Jesus, a fact that happened in history, and the announcement of Jesus Christ personally recognized as the living Word of God, pronounced on history.

The fruits of his testimony will scatter like seeds in the wind fallen on good ground. Or they will be distributed to feed the hungry for truth, love, and meaning for life. The time of Easter will inevitably come. Jails, hammers, nails, knives, and bullets always seem to wreck everything, but in reality they always arrive late, for the word is already sown in many generous and fruitful wombs. These are the wombs of men and women who bear the testimony and bring it to fruition, or the earth that opens its fruitful womb to receive the seed that will later become a leafy and turgid fruit tree. The extirpated prophet had no apparent success in his purposes, but was fruitful in the womb of history where the novelty of God's plan is alive without recess or rest.

The community, which is an ecclesial cell, shows what the whole church is called to be. Their martyrdom is:

- A call for attention to what is essential. It is not so much the rules, the irreproachable and radical following of the principles and what is written in the books and records of the religious order or congregation. The essential thing is to live the gospel, to be a group of people who closely and radically follow the lifestyle of Jesus. And so they are open and ready to develop loving and dialogical relationships with all people, cultures, and traditions. They draw attention to love, unique in deserving faith[2] and unique in indicating the identity and belonging of those communities. In the midst of the secularity and plurality of today's world, Christianity is called to enter into this diversity and to give its witness ever since. This is the case with the testimony of both communities.

- A testimony that surprises the world. Why did both communities give a testimony that shook public opinion and surprised the world? In part, it surprised everyone where this testimony resonated. It came from a sociopolitical-economic and not-so-ecclesial context, in the case of the Jesuits. It came from a multi-religious context or even from a society with theocratic characteristics, as was the case with the monks of Tibhirine. The issues that triggered the radical

2. Balthasar, *L'amour seul est digne de foi.*

engagement of both communities were secular, not theological or religious. At least not directly. In the case of the Jesuits this was clearly apparent. The community, from its charisma and mysticism, wanted to be an instance of prophetic denunciation against an oppressive and unjust government, following in the footsteps of Monsignor Romero, also a martyr, nine years before the Jesuits. And this mysticism, with its expected consequences of liberating El Salvador's poor and oppressed, came from the academic, secular, though Christian-inspired space. From the university areopagus,[3] the Jesuits turned their study, research, teaching, and extension activities to transform this unfair context in which they lived. But they also allied to this the insertion between poor communities on the periphery. Almost all of them worked with these communities scattered on the outskirts of the capital of El Salvador and from there preached the Gospel and helped transform reality.

- The work of the monks of Tibhirine had slightly different characteristics. Their space was not a university but a monastery. However, they made this explicitly religious space a place of openness to the poorer communities in the neighborhood. They provided services of all kinds, not just religious. Among them, we should highlight the medical services that the tireless and admirable Frère Luc performed, sometimes treating more than 150 patients a day.[4] For his part, Prior Christian de Chergé created a movement involving religious and laity, Christians and Muslims, to pray and work in peacebuilding. Acting on something religious (prayer) but also universal (peacebuilding), he lived and testified that it was possible to transform the society in which he lived. And all this was done in absolute respect for the other religion that collaborated with him in this peacebuilding. The *Lien de paix* (Peace Link) group was made up of Christians and Islamists who together prayed and thought about a way to advance peace in the country.[5]

- A communal liturgy of giving of life for the glory of God and his kingdom. In fact, the martyrdom of the two communities, expected and somewhat prepared by them, has the status of a liturgy. Such was

3. Cf. the encyclical of John Paul II, *Redemptoris Missio*, where the university is counted among the new Areopagus of modernity.

4. Kiser, *Passion for l'Algeria*.

5. Ray, *Christian de Chergé*.

martyrdom generally in the early days of Christianity: a public event with characteristics of celebration. The martyrs were exposed in visible spaces and their execution open to the whole population, such as the Roman circus, or the city streets, or the roads on the outskirts of the cities. They were oblations of the liturgy of the Roman Empire, which preached the worship of the emperor. On the side of the martyrs, they accepted death for their convictions and, above all, for their felt need to bear witness.[6] In fact, the martyrs were committed to making visible, in the world and in the eyes of all, Jesus and what he represented, that is, the kingdom of God already here and now. Their lives were lived for that purpose and their deaths are a consequence of it.[7] This liturgy is indeed eucharistic, for the martyrs and their testimony are food for all who can witness their death as well as for those who kill them. One can recall here Ignatius, bishop of Antioch, a second-century martyr, who calls the guards leading him to the execution "ferocious beasts" similar to the animals in the arena in which he will be killed, while declaring his desire to be "food," understanding himself in eucharistic terms. The effect, the consequence of this will be "the distribution of Christ in person to the population."[8] In our case, there are the communities themselves who live this Eucharistic vocation, which is liturgically made visible and actually realized. It is worth remembering what the monk Christophe Lebreton writes about the configuration of his community, using the Greek word that describes the liturgical moment of consecration, when the Spirit transforms the species into the body and blood of Christ for the food of all the people: *epiclesis*.[9]

This is what these two communities teach us today:

A way to be truly human. There is profound anthropological significance in the testimony of these two religious communities that seal their lives and their act by martyrial surrender. In a historical and cultural moment where human beings seem to have become synonymous with owning, consuming, and seeking happiness in the acquisition of more and more

---

6. Young, *In Procession.*

7. Young, *In Procession*, 6.

8. Young, *In Procession*, 8. The author quotes Rom 4:1–2, and refers to the letter of Ignatius of Antioch to the Romans.

9. As Christophe Lebreton uses this term, by us already quoted here.

material objects, they teach that human beings are, on the contrary, giving, offering, opening to the other, and committed to it, being faithful until the end to that delivery. In this sense, more than consuming, being human is "being consumed."[10]

Human life is called to be a given, delivered life. This reminds Christian de Chergé constantly of his community. Their lives have already been given. What could happen at that moment when the threat of death was prowling would be no more than the direct consequence of consistency with this delivery already made. Life is created not to be admired or worshipped but to serve others, to help others, even those of another religion, of another tradition, of another culture, and to have more open ways to be truly human. So it is with the Jesuit community, which understood itself as existing to bring down the poor from the cross. Its story was the story of "a university's efforts to help El Salvador's" crucified people "come down from the cross, supporting their efforts to build a society in which everyone had the opportunity to share a future where dignity, love, compassion, and sanity might prevail."[11]

A Christological path. In fact, what the testimony of the two communities says with their martyrdom is that to be human is to be governed by otherness, by the other who, from the epiphany of his/her face, challenges and calls Christian de Chergé, a profound connoisseur of Levinas, who applied and taught this to his confreres. Ellacuría, brilliant philosopher, introduced this centrality of otherness through the concept of "reality" from his master Zubiri.[12] It is a reality to be borne, to take upon one's shoulders, announcing the kingdom of God there.

In fact, it is the way of Jesus Christ himself that is retraced through those who follow him. Both communities are Christian and even Catholic. But they are open to all the diversities and differences that cross their path. UCA serves the poor of El Salvador who are, it is true—at least when the community lived and acted there—mostly Catholic. However, it is not recognized as such by its own countrymen, who do not hesitate to write on the walls that in order to be a patriot one must kill the priests who desire the revolution that would change the lives of Salvadorans. Surely many non-Catholics had received welcome, listening, and dialogue within the UCA. And certainly there were many non-believers who dialogued there, as is

10. Cavanaugh, *On Being Consumed.*

11. Lassalle-Klein, *Blood and Ink,* 23.

12. Vigil, *Bajar de la Cruz.*

often the case in academic circles, where freedom of belonging and expression must always be an undisputed fact. In any case, the murdered Jesuits are intellectuals who have not locked themselves in the familiar environment of their identity. They were not researchers who were restricted to their labs or teachers who only worked in the classroom. They met the different, the poor, in their communities, and learned from them a new way of thinking, of celebrating, and of living, at last. They entered into communion with otherness, as did Jesus of Nazareth, who included at the table of his kingdom those who were considered without God, by their state of health, by their birth, their gender, and by their political or religious belonging.

The Trappist community of Tibhirine goes this way even more explicitly. Being a Catholic contemplative community, they do not hesitate to meet the Muslims and their religion. And they do this in the style of Jesus, who opens up and allows foreigners to not be considered idolaters, such as the Syro-Phoenician or the Samaritan;[13] as well as those who are touched by impure and sinful women without fear of contamination;[14] those who exalt the behavior of publicans who, from their difference, can teach those who consider themselves elect and hold the Lord's preferences;[15] and those who open the doors of his kingdom to anyone who seeks God with a sincere heart. Opening the space of his monastery, he prays for Muslims to pray there, meeting those brothers of another faith to pray with them and welcoming them into their personal and communitarian space. Giving their lives to the end, the monks of Tibhirine bear witness to a radical following of Jesus. By opening themselves to the difference of others in their faith, they are more than ever followers of this Jesus to whom they gave their lives and whose following they wished to live and encouraged others to live. It is then an inclusive follow-up that the two communities live and transmit, proclaiming a Gospel not closed, but open and inclusive, as was, in its time, the Good News announced by Jesus of Nazareth.

A path to be a church. Both communities show equally through their witness an ecclesiological path. That is, they teach and seal with their blood a way, a style of being church that can be the teaching for the whole church. In the case of UCA, the proposed church model has already been linked to a chain that was a majority in Latin America throughout the 1970s and 1980s. The Jesuit community of El Salvador was aligned with this project

13. Cf. Matt 15:21–28; Mark 7:24–30. See also Luke 10:25–37.
14. Luke 7:36–50.
15. Cf. Luke 18:9–14 or John 19:1.

and this church model. In other words, it is a church that conceives itself more horizontal and less vertical, more people-centered—a category established by the Second Vatican Council in the dogmatic constitution *Lumen Gentium*, which sees the church as people of God—than pyramidal, centered on the clergy and episcopate. Moreover, it is a church geared to the poor as its pastoral and missionary priority. A church that wants to incarnate itself among the poor and from there, from this place, help them to be artisans of their liberation and fight their poverty. This church continues to exist in Latin America, fueled by popular Bible readings, pilgrimages, and walks that draw attention to the plight of the excluded and denunciations of injustices committed by various autocratic and elitist governments. Some of the prophets were murdered, such as members of the UCA community, several of them were punished, curtailed in their right to write and to teach. But the seeds they have sown continue to sprout and slowly bring on the dawn of a new day, which may be late, but it will come. The hope of the people is also maintained by the memory of these martyrs, showing a committed and incarnate church with the people.

The model of the church revealed by the Tibhirine community also has the element of solidarity with the poor and excluded. Clearly it was out of solidarity with these disinherited progressors that the monks did not leave where they were, hoping to help and protect with their permanence those who were also threatened by the violence that prevailed in that place, but could not retreat or leave. Above all, they show a model of the church that is humbly conscious of not holding the monopoly of truth, but sharing it with the other traditions, which name God with other names. The monastery of Tibhirine was a trans-religious ecclesial community, which deeply lived its Christian and Catholic identity, but was permeable to all the richness of dialogue with another tradition. It was a community that allowed itself to be shaped by its relationship with these other traditions and religions. Their difference was a constitutive part of their identity and gave them the striking feature of the diversity in which their ecclesial profile consisted. Today we see other examples and cases following Tibhirine's model, at the same time renewing and reconfiguring it. We can remember here the case of Taizé, an ecumenical monastery founded by Brother Roger of Taizé, which attracts thousands of young people worldwide and expands its foundations in various parts of the world. We can also remember initiatives such as the monastery of Bose in Italy, whose prior, Enzo Bianchi, is one of the exponents of ecumenical dialogue. In addition, we can remember the monastery founded by the Italian Jesuit Paolo dall'Oglio in Syria, which brought together for prayer and sharing people from the three monotheistic traditions. His mysterious disappearance several years ago does not prevent the seeds he sowed, inspiring him to found that place of trans-religious prayer, to continue to bear fruit in various parts of the Middle East and to universally radiate the spirit of interreligious dialogue. The church that lived, suffered, and died in the monastic community in Tibhirine is still alive. It's not over. And the spirit that inspired it remains present in the Church of Christ, which is ever more open, in the last pontificates and in a special way in the pontificate of Pope Francis, toward universal and borderless communion.

Bibliography

Books

Antoine, Ch. *Le sang des justes. Mgr Romero, les jesuites et l' Amerique Latine*. Paris: DDB, 2000.

Ashley, John Matthew. "Contemplation in the Action of Justice: Ignacio Ellacuría and Ignatian Spirituality." In *Love that Produces Hope: The Thought of Ignacio Ellacuría*, edited by Kevin Burke and Robert Lassalle-Klein, 144–67. Collegeville, MN: Liturgical/Michael Glazier, 2006.

Bahder, G. *Tibhirine: une relation a Dieu et aux autres*. Montdescats: Bellefontaine, 2010.

Balthasar, Hans Urs. *L'amour seul est digne de foi*. Paris: Parole et Silence, 1999.

Batstone, D., ed. *New Visions for the Americas. Religious Engagement and Social Transformation*. Minneapolis: Fortress, 1993.

Beirne, Charles J., SJ. *Jesuit Education and Social Change in El Salvador*. London: Garland, 1996.

Belisle, P. D. *The Language of Silence. The Changing Face of Monastic Solitude*. New York: Orbis, 2003.

Bertrand, Dominique. *Un corps pour l'Esprit*. Paris: DDB, collection Christus, 1970.

Besselaar, José Van Den. *António Vieira: o homem, a obra, as ideias*. Lisbon: ICALP, 1981.

Bingemer, Maria Clara. *Dom Oscar Romero: Mártir da libertação*. 1st ed. Rio de Janeiro/ São Paulo: PUC-Rio/Santuário, 2012.

———. *Em tudo amar e servir. Mística trinitária e práxis cristã em Santo Inácio de Loyola*. São Paulo: Loyola, 1990.

———. *Latin American Theology: Roots and Branches*. New York: Orbis, 2017.

———. *Violência e religião: Cristianismo, Judaismo e Islamismo em confronto e dialogo* (*Violence and Religion: Christianity, Judaism and Islam in Confrontation and Dialogue*). São Paulo: PUC-Rio, 2001.

Boff, Clodovis. "Igreja militante de Joao Paulo II e o capitalismo triunfante" (The Militant Church of John Paul II and Triumphant Capitalism). In *Doutrina Social da Igreja e Teologia da Libertação*, edited by Francisco Ivern and Maria Clara Bingemer. São Paulo: Loyola, 1994.

———. *Teologia de pé no chão*. Petrópolis: Vozes, 1984.

———. *Teologia e Prática Teologia do Político e suas mediações*. Petrópolis: Vozes, 1978.

Boff, Leonardo. *Church, Charism, and Power: Liberation Theology and the Institutional Church.* London: SCM, 1985.

———. *Igreja, carisma e poder: ensaios de eclesiologia militante.* Petrópolis: Vozes, 1984.

Broderick, J. F., and V. A. Lapomarda. "Jesuits." In vol. 7, *New Catholic Encyclopedia,* 779–81. Gale Virtual Reference Library. 2nd ed. Detroit: Gale, 2003.

Buechner, F. *The Faces of Jesus: A Life Story.* Brewster, MA: Paraclete, 2005.

Buelta, Gonzalez. *Bajar al encuentro de Dios. Vida de oración entre los pobre.* Santander: Sal Terrae, 1992.

Burke, K. F. *The Ground Beneath the Cross: The Theology of Ignacio Ellacuría.* Washington, DC: Georgetown University Press, 2000.

Burke, K. F., and Burke Sullivan. *The Ignatian Tradition.* Minnesota: Liturgical, 2009.

Burke, K. F., and R. Lassalle-Klein, eds. *Love that Produces Hope: The Thought of Ignacio Ellacuría.* Collegeville, MN: Liturgical, 2006.

Cailler, Alain. *Une anthropologie du don. Le Tiers paradigme.* Paris: Poche, 2007. As in Jean-Luc Marion. *Etant donné. Essai sur une phénoménologie de la donation.* 3rd ed. Paris: PUF, 2005.

Calvez, Yves. *Foi et justice.* Paris: DDB, 1985.

Camus, Albert. *L'Étranger.* Collection Folio. Paris: Éditions Gallimard, 1942.

———. *Le premier homme. Paris: Gallimard,* 1994.

Cardenal, Fernando. *Sacerdote em la revolución.* Manágua: Anamá, 2008.

Cardenal, R. *Historia de una esperanza. Vida de Rutilio Grande.* San Salvador: UCA Editores, 1985.

Cardenal, R., et al. *Ignacio Ellacuría intellectual, filosofo y teologo.* Valencia: ADG-N Libros, 2012.

———. *Ignacio Ellacuría: el hombre, el pensador, el Cristiano.* Bilbao: EGA, 1994.

Cavanaugh, William. *On Being Consumed: Economics and Christian Desire.* Grand Rapids: Eerdmans, 2008.

Ceruti Guldberg, H. *Universidad y cambio social (Los jesuitas en El Salvador).* Ciudad de México: Magna Terra, 1990.

Chalier, Catherine. *La trace de l'infini—Emmanuel Levinas et la source hébraïque.* Paris: Cerf, 2002.

Chanteur, Janine. *Chronique d'une enfance meurtrie: Les petits enfants de Job.* Paris, Seuil, 1990.

Chenu, B. *Sept vies pour Dieu et l' Algerie.* Paris: Bayard, 1996.

Chergé, Christian de. *Dieu pour tout jour: Chapitres de Père Christian de Chergé à la communauté de Tibhirine, 1986–1996.* Collection Les Cahiers de Tibhirine Montjoyer: Abbaye Notre-Dame d'Aiguebelle, 2004.

———. *La esperanza invencible.* Buenos Aires/Ciudad de México: Lumen, 2007.

———. *L'Autre que nous attendons: homélies de père, 1970–1996.* Collection Les cahiers de Tibhirine. Série Paroles; 2nd ed. Godewaersvelde: Éditions de Bellefontaine, 2009.

———. *L'invincible Esperance.* Edited and compiled by Bruno Chenu. Paris: Bayard, 1997.

———. *Les vies des saints du Poitou et des personnages d' une eminente piete qui son nes ou qui ont vecu dans cette province.* Nantes: Ed. J-M Williamson, 1994.

Christoph, Arnold J. *Why Forgive?* Farmington: Plough Publishing, 2000.

Clement, A. N., et al. *Le Verbe s' est fait frère. Christian de Chergé et le dialogue islamo-chretien.* Paris: Bayard, 2010.

Code of Canon Law. Vatican.va, n.d. https://www.vatican.va/archive/cod-iuris-canonici/cic_index_en.html.

Coleman, J. A., and W. F. Ryan. *Globalization and Catholic Social Thought.* Maryknoll, NY: Orbis, 2005.

Constituições da Companhia de Jesus e Normas Complementares. São Paulo: Loyola, 2014.

Craigo-Snell, S. *Silence, Love and Death: Saying "Yes" to God in the Theology of Karl Rahner.* Milwaukee: Marquette University Press, 2008.

D' Escrivain, E. *Un monastere cistercien en terre d' Islam? Notre-Dame de l'Atlas au Maroc.* Paris: Cerf, 2010.

Davies, N., and M. Conway. *World Christianity in the Twentieth Century.* London: SCM, 2008.

Del Ville, J-P. *Mysticisms et politiques. Une lecture de Bernard de Clairvaux, Claire d' Assise, Julienne de Cornillon, Edith Stein, Etty Hillesum et des sept peres trappistes de Tibhirine.* Bruxelles: Lumen Vitae, 2005.

Derwahl, F. *Le dernier moine de Tibhirine.* Paris: Albin Michel, 2012.

Deslandres, D. "Examplo aeque ut verbo." In *The Jesuits: Cultures, Sciences and the Arts, 1540–1773,* edited by J. O'Malley, 258–73. Vol 1. Toronto: University of Toronto Press, 1999.

Desroche, Henri. *Évolution de l'Image de la Mort dans la Société contemporaine et le Discours religieux des Églises* [actes du 4e colloque du center de sociologie du protestantisme de l'université des sciences strasbourg humains (3–5 October 1974)], 202–3.

Donahue, A. "Cenobites." In vol. 3 of *New Catholic Encyclopedia,* 334. 2nd ed. Detroit: Gale, 2003. https://cvdvn.files.wordpress.com/2018/05/new-catholic-encyclopedia-vol-3.pdf.

———. "Hermits." In vol. 6 of *New Catholic Encyclopedia,* 799–800. 2nd ed. Detroit: Gale, 2003. https://cvdvn.files.wordpress.com/2018/05/new-catholic-encyclopedia-vol-6.pdf.

Dubay, Th. *Caring: A Biblical Theology of Community.* New Jersey: Denville, 1973.

Dulles, Avery. *Models of the Church.* New York: Image, 1991.

Dupont, Jacques. *Marthe et Marie: le service et l' ecoute, in Pourquoi des paraboles?.* Paris: Cerf, 1977.

———. *Pourquoi des paraboles? La methode parabolique de Jesus.* Paris: Cerf, 1977.

Eglash, Albert. "Beyond Restitution: Creative Restitution." In *Restitution in Criminal Justice,* edited by Joe Hudson and Burt Galaway, 91–129. Lexington, MA: Lexington Books, 1977.

Ellacuría, I. *Conversion de la Iglesia al Reino de Dios. Para anunciarlo y realizarlo en la historia.* Santander: Sal Terrae, 1984.

———. *El compromise politico de la filosofia en America Latina.* Bogota: El Buho, 1994.

———. *Escritos teologicos.* San Salvador: UCA Editores, vols. I and II (2000), vols. III and IV (2002).

———. *Essays on History, Liberation, and Salvation.* NY: Orbis, 2013.

———. *Fe y justicia.* Bilbao: DDB, 1999.

———. *Filosofia de la realidad histórica.* Madrid: Trotta, 1991.

———. *Freedom Made Flesh: The Mission of Christ and His Church.* Maryknoll, NY: Orbis, 1976.

———. *Liberacion mision y charisma de la Iglesia latinoamericana, document 5, MIECJECI.* Lima, marzo 1975.

Ellacuría, I. and J. C. Scannone. *Para una filosofia desde America Latina.* Colección Universitas Philosophica. Bogota: Universidad Javeriana, 1992.

Fadini, G. *Ignacio Ellacuría*. Collana Novecento Teologico. Brescia: Morcelliana, 2012.

Festugière, A. J. *Contemplation et vie contemplative selon Platon*. Paris: Vrin, 1950.

The Formula of the Instituto da Companhia de Jesus (The Institute's Formula). The pontiff approved orally on September 3, 1539.

Gimbernat, J., and C. Gomez, eds. *La passion por la libertad, Homenaje a Ignacio Ellacuría*. Estella: Verbo Divino, 1994.

Gorce, Bernard. Reportagem publicada no jornal La Croix, September 5, 2010. Disponível em: https://www.la-croix.com/Religion/Actualite/L-histoire-des-moines-de-Tibhirine-2010-09-05-578037.

Grün, Anselm. *Benedict of Nursia: His Message for Today*. Translated by Linda M. Maloney. Collegeville, MN: Liturgical, 2006.

Guitton, René. *Si nous nous taisons: Le martyre de moines de Tibhirine*. 2nd ed. Paris: Calmann-Lévy, 2009.

Gutierrez, Gustavo. *Teología de la Liberación. Perspectivas*. Lima: CEP, 1971.

———. *A Theology of Liberation: History, Politics, and Salvation*. Translated and edited by Sister Caridad Inda and John Eagleson. Maryknoll, NY: Orbis, 1973.

———. *A Theology of Liberation: History, Politics, and Salvation*. Revised edition. Translated and edited by Sister Caridad Inda and John Eagleson. Maryknoll, NY: Orbis, 1988.

Häring, Hermann. *Apostar no que é bom: superando a violência em nome das religiões*. In: Concilium, fasc.272, v. 33. Petrópolis: Vozes, 1997/4, 122 [698]–143 [719].

Hasset, J., and H. Lacey. *Towards a Society that Serves Its People: The Intellectual Contribution of El Salvador's Murdered Jesuits*. Washington, DC: Georgetown University Press, 1991.

Hennelly, Alfred T., ed. *Liberation Theology: A Documentary History*. Maryknoll, NY: Orbis, 1990.

Hennelly, Alfred T., and J. Langan, eds. *Human Rights in the Americas: The Struggle for Consensus*. Washington, DC: Georgetown University Press, 1982.

Henning, Christophe. *Christian de Chergé, monk of Tibhirine, foreword by Jean-Marie Rouart*. Paris: Mediapaul, 2014.

———. *Frere Luc, la biographie: moine, medecin et martyr a Tibhirine*. Paris: Bayard, 2011.

———. *Petite vie des moines de Tibhirine*. Paris: DDB, 2006.

Hillery, G. A. *The Monastery: A Study in Freedom, Love and Community*. Westport, CT: Praeger, 1992.

Hillesum, Etty. *Diarios*. Lisbon: Assirio and Alvim, 2007.

Hogan Closkey, P. and J. P. Hogan. *Romero's Legacy: The Call to Peace and Justice*. Plymouth, UK: Rowman & Littlefield, 2007.

Holztrattner, M., and C. Sedmak, eds. *Humanities and Option for the Poor*. Munster: LIT Verlag, 2005.

Idígoras, Jose Ignacio Tellechea. *Inácio de Loyola, Alone and On Foot*. São Paulo: Loyola, 1996.

Ignatius, St. *Autobiography: Dictated to Fr. Luis Gonçalves da Câmara*. Brazilian ed. São Paulo: Loyola, 2010.

Instituto de Derechos Humanos de la UCA, Caso jesuítas. Instituto de Estudios Centroamericanos, 2000.

Instituto de Estudios Centroamericanos y el Rescate. *The Jesuit Assassinations: The Writings of Ellacuría, Martin Baro and Segundo Montes, with a Chronology of the Investigation*. Kansas City: Sheed and Ward, 1990.

Ivern, Francisco. *O neoliberalismo da América Latina. Carta dos Superiores Provinciais Jesuítas na América Latina.* Documento de Trabalho. São Paulo: Loyola, 1996.

Jean Olwen, M. *Christian de Chergé and the Atlas Martyrs, Holy See.* Catholic Truth Society, 2003.

Jennings, Th. W., Jr. *Transforming Atonement: A Political Theology of the Cross.* Minneapolis: Fortress, 2009.

Jerez, Cesar. "Speech of the UCA Dean." Envio: Managua, April 1990 (DIAL, n. 1505, June 21, 1990).

Johnson, W. *Encyclopedia of Monastycism.* Chicago: Fitsroy Dearborn, 2000.

Ker, Ian. *The Achievement of John Henry Newman.* Notre Dame: Notre Dame University Press, 1990.

Kiser, J. *The Monks of Tibhirine: Faith, Love and Terror in Algeria.* New York: St. Martin's Griffin, 2002.

―――. *Passion pour l'Algérie: les moines de Thibirine.* Montrouge: Nouvelle Cité, 2006.

Koraichi, R. *Les sept dormants. Sept livres en homage aux 7 moines de Tibhirine.* Lucon: Actes Sud, 2004.

Krokus, Christian S. *The Theology of Louis Massignon: Christ, Islam and the Church.* Washington: The Catholic University of America Press, 2017.

Kung, H., and J. Moltmann. *A Council for Peace.* Concilium 195. London: T & T Clark, 1988.

Lassalle-Klein, R., et al. *Blood and Ink: Ignacio Ellacuría, Jon Sobrino and the Jesuit Martyrs of the University of Central America.* New York: Orbis, 2014.

Lassausse, Jean-Marie, and Christophe Henning. *Le jardinier de Tibhibine.* Paris: Bayard, 2010.

Lebreton, Christophe. *Aime jusqu' au bout du feu.* Paris: Monte-Cristo, 2000.

―――. *Moine de Tibhirine.* Journal: Tibhirine 1993–1996: le soufflé du don. Paris: Bayard, 1999.

Lee, M. E. *Bearing the Way of Salvation.* New York: Crossroad, 2009.

―――. *Transforming Realities: Christian Discipleship in the Soteriology of Ignacio Ellacuría.* South Bend: Notre Dame, 2005.

Levinas, Emmanuel. *Altérité et transcendance.* Montpellier: Fata Morgana, 1995.

―――. *Autrement qu'etre ou au-delà de l'essence.* La Haye: Martinus Nijhoff, 1974.

―――. *De Outro Modo que Ser ou para lá da Essência.* Lisbon: Center of Philosophy of the University of Lisbon, 2011.

―――. *Entre nous. Essais sur le penser à l'autre, Paris, Grasset, 1991; Dificile liberté. Essai sur le Judaïsme.* Paris: Albin Michel, 1963; 2nd ed, 1976.

―――. *Ethique et infini. Dialogues avec Philippe Nemo.* Paris: Librairie Arthème Fayard et Radio France, 1982.

―――. *Totalidade e infinito.* Lisboa: Edições 70, 1988.

―――. *Un Dieu homme? in Entre nous. Essais sur le penser à l'autre.* Paris: Grasset, 1991.

Lois, J. *Teología de la Liberación. Opción por los Pobres.* Madri: IEPALA, 1988.

Loriente Pardillo, J. L. *Ignacio Ellacuría.* Salamanca: Kadmos, 2004.

Mainwaring, Scott. *Igreja Católica e Política no Brasil (1916–1985).* São Paulo: Brasiliense, 2004.

Martin, M. *El Padre Arrupe: testigo y profeta.* San Salvador: Centro Monsenor Romero, 2007.

Mason, M. E., *Active Life and Contemplative Life: A Study of the Concepts from Plato to the Present.* Milwaukee: Marquette University Press, 1961.

Masson, Robert. *Tibhirine: les veilleurs de l''Atlas*. Paris: Du Cerf, 1998.

Maynard, J. O. *Christian de Chergé and the Atlas Martyrs*. Vatican: Catholic Truth Society, 2003.

McDermott, Robert. "Consecrated Life." In vol. 4, *New Catholic Encyclopedia*, 155. 2nd ed. Detroit: Gale, 2003.

McGovern, Arthur F. *Liberation Theology and Its Critics: Toward an Assessment*. Eugene, OR: Wipf and Stock, 2009.

Melià, Bartomeu, and Liane Maria Nagel. *Guaraníes y Jesuítas en tiempo de las Misiones: una bibliografía didáctica*. Asunción/Rio Grande do Sul: CEPAG/URI, 1995.

Metz, J. B. and E. Schillebeeckx, eds. *Martyrdom Today*, Concilium. New York: Seabury, 1983.

Metz, J. B. and J. P. Jossua. *Christianity and Socialism*. Concilium v. 105. New York: Seabury, 1977.

Miguez Bonino, J. *Faces of Jesus: Latin American Christologies*. New York: Orbis, 1977.

Minassian, M. D. *Frere Christophe Lebreton moine de Tibhirine. De l' enfant bien-aime a l'homme tout donne*. Mont des Cats: Editions Bellefontaine, 2009.

Monchanin, Jules, et al. *Theologie et spiritualité missionnaires*. Paris: Beauchesne, 1985.

Monges da Abadia Nossa Senhora do Novo Mundo. Histórico da Ordem Cisterciense da Estrita Observância (OCSO). http://voxsilencio.blogspot.com.br/2009/03/trapistas-ordem-cisterciense-da-estrita.html.

Moubarac,Youakim, and Guy Harpigny. *O Islã na reflexão teológica cristã contemporânea*. Concilium, fasc.116, n. X. Petrópolis: Vozes, 1976/6.

Nephew, Jon. *Jesucristo liberador: Lectura histórica-teológica de Jesús de Nazaret*. San Salvador: UCA, 1991.

Neuhaus,R. J. *The Eternal Pity. Reflections on Dying*. Notre Dame: University of Notre Dame Press, 2000.

Okure, T., et al. *Rethinking Martyrdom*. Concilium 1. London: SCM, 2003.

Olivera, B. *How Far to Follow? The Martyrs of Atlas*. Petersham, MA: St. Bede's, 1997.

O'Malley, John. *The First Jesuits*. Cambridge: Harvard University Press, 1993.

———. *To Travel to Any Part of the World: Jerónimo Nadal and the Jesuit Vocation*. Studies in the Spirituality of Jesuits 16.2, 1984.

Paiva, José Pedro. *Padre Antonio Vieira, 1608-1697: Bibliografia*. Lisbon: Biblioteca Nacional, 1999.

Palumbo, Cecília, and Alejandro Bertolini. *La casa en el Puente: Christophe Lebreton huésped de fronteras*. Buenos Aires: Agape Libros, 2017.

Pascal, Blaise. *Pensées diverses VIII*—Fragment n° 3 / 6--Papier original: RO 159-3. Copies manuscrites du XVIIe s. C1 n° 189 p. 427 v° / C2 p. 399-399 v° (copie de Pierre Guerrier). Éditions de Port-Royal: Chap. XXVIII - Pensées Chrestiennes: 1669 et janv. 1670 p. 271 / 1678 n° 72 p. 264. Éditions savantes: Faugère II, 190, VI / Havet XXIV.46 / Brunschvicg 593 / Tourneur p. 136-1 / Le Guern 672 / Lafuma 822 (série XXX) / Sellier 663.

Peliccia, G., and G. Rocca. *Dizionario degli istituti di perfezione*. Roma: Paoline, 1983.

Pelikan, J. *The Idea of the University: A Reexamination*. New Haven: Yale University Press, 1992.

Peyriguère, Albert. *Aussi loin que l'amour: lettres du Maroc (1933-1957). Présentation de L.-Francis Hardy*. Paris: Cerf, 1970.

Place, François. *Os Cistercienses: documentos primitivos*. São Paulo: Musa, 1997.

Pope, S. J. *Hope and Solidarity. Jon Sobrino's Challenge to Christian Theology*. New York: Orbis, 2008.

Pratt, Lonni Collins, and Daneil Homan, OSB. *Benedict's Way: An Ancient Monk's Insights for a Balanced Life*. Chicago: Loyola, 2001.

Quinson, Henry C. *Optimisme naïf ou invincible espérance ?: Christian de Chergé selon John Kiser*. Colloque Tibhirine de l'ISTR de Marseille, samedi 5 mars 2005. http://henry. quinson.pagesperso-orange.fr/Colloque%20ISTR%20Tibhirine%20Chemin%20 de%20dialogue.pdf.

Rahner, Karl. *Curso Fundamental da fé*. Sao Paulo: Paulinas, 1989.

Rault, Claude. *Désert, ma cathédrale*. Paris: Desclée de Brouwer, 2008.

Ray, Marie-Christine. *Christian de Chergé, prieur de Tibhirine*. Paris: Bayard, 1998.

———. *Le temoignage de Tibhirine: un chemin de rencontre entre chretiens et musulmans*. Chemins de Dialogue 13. L'Autre que nous attendons: Vingt ans ce dialogue interreligieux monastique, 17–30. Marseille, 1999. http://icm.catholique.fr/pdf/ CdD-13.pdf.

Riccardi, Andrea. *As religiões no século XX entre a violência e o diálogo*. Concilium, fasc.272, v. 33. Petrópolis: Vozes, 1997/4.

Ritchie, J. *Ma tete a couper*. Paris: Bourgoism, 1990.

Rosillo Martinez, A. *Los derechos humanos desde el pensamiento de Ignacio Ellacuría*. Madrid: Dykinsobn, 2009.

Salenson, Christian. *Christian de Chergé. Une theologie de l' Esperance*. Paris: Bayard, 2009.

———. *Du bom usage de l'échelle mysticism*. In Le Verbe s'est fait frère: *Christian de Chergé et le dialogue islamo-chrétien*, Anne-Noëlle Clément, et al., 35–43. Paris: Bayard, 2010.

———. *Prier 15 jours avec Christian de Chergé: prieur des moines de Tibhirine*. Montrouge: Nouvelle cité, impr. 2006. Collection Prier 15 hours n° 102.

Salenson, Christian, and Christian de Chergé. *A Theology of Hope*. Collegeville, MN: Liturgical, 2012.

Samour, H., *Voluntad de liberacion. El pensamiento filosofico de Ignacio Ellacuría*. El Salvador: UCA Editores, 2002.

Schumacher, Frère Jean-Pierre. *Thibhirine . . . Fès . . . Midelt . . .* http://www.arccis.org/ downloads/tibhirinefesmidelt.pdf.

Sement de Frutos, J. A. *Ellacuría y los derechos humanos*. Bilbao: Desclee de Brouwer, 1998.

Serbin, Kenneth P. *Dialogos na sombra*. Rio de Janeiro: Companhia das Letras, 2001.

Shea, Philip. "Religious (Men and Women)." In vol. 12, *New Catholic Encyclopedia*, 88. 2nd ed. Detroit: Gale, 2003.

Sobrino, Jon. *Christology in Latin America*. Petrópolis: Vozes, 1982.

———. *Ignacio Ellacuría, in Bajar de la cruz al Pueblo crucificado*. San Salvador: Centro Monseñor Romero, 2001.

———. *Jesus in Latin America: Essay from the Victims*. São Paulo: Loyola, 2000.

Sobrino, Jon, and R. Alvarado. *Ignacio Ellacuría: Aquella libertad esclarecida*. El Salvador: UCA editors, 1999.

Sodré, Olga Regina Frugoli. "Monges em diálogo a caminho do absoluto: estudo psicossocial do diálogo inter-religioso monástico." PhD diss., Pontifícia Universidade Católica do Rio de Janeiro, 2005.

Sols Lucia, J. *La teologia historica de Ignacio Ellacuría*. Madrid: Trotta, 1999.

————. *The Legacy of Ignacio Ellacuría Ten Years After Martyrdom*. Cristianisme e Justicia 86. San Cugat, 1999.

Susin, L. C., et al. *A Different World Is Possible*. Concilium 5. London: SCM, 2004.

Susini, Mirella. *Il martirio Cristiano esperienza di incontro con Cristo. Testimonianze dei primi tre secoli*. Bologna: EDB, 2002.

————. *I martiri di Tibhirini*. Bologna: Edizioni Dehoniane, 2005.

————. *"Io vivo rischiando per Te": Christophe Lebreton trappista, martire del XX secolo*. Bologna: Edizioni Dehoniane, 2008.

Swan, L. *The Benedictine Tradition*. Minnesotta: Liturgical, 2007.

Teixeira, F. *Buscadores do diálogo*. São Paulo: Paulinas, 2012.

Tepedino, Ana Maria. *As discípulas de Jesus*. Petrópolis: Vozes, 1990.

Theobald, Ch. *Presences d' Evangile. Lire les Evangiles et l' Apocalypse en Algerie et ailleurs*. Paris: L' Atelier, 2011.

Thurian, Max. *Tradition et renouveau dans l' Esprit*. Paris: Taizé, 1977.

Van Nispen tot Sevenaer, Christian. *Chrétiens et musulmans: frères devant Dieu ?*. Paris: Les Éditions de l'"Atelier; Les Éditions Ouvrières, 2009.

Veilleux, Armand. *A Importância da comunidade monástica e a Igreja na vida contemplativa*. Conferência pronunciada na Bélgica na Abadia de Gethsemani a 25 de julho de 1996. http://users.skynet.be/bs775533/Armand/wri/gethsem-por.htm.

Vigil, José Maria, ed. *Bajar de la Cruz a los Pobres: Cristología de la Liberación*. https://servicioskoinonia.org/LibrosDigitales/LDK/ASETTBajarDeLaCruz2.pdf.

Whitfield, T. *Pagando el precio. Ignacio Ellacuría y el asesinato de los jesuitas en El Salvador*. San Salvador: UCA Editores, 1998.

————. *Paying the Price. Ignacio Ellacuría and the Murdered Jesuits of El Salvador*. Philadelphia: Temple University Press, 1995.

Wilfred, F., and O. Beozzo, eds. *Frontier violations*, Concilium 2. Maryknoll, NY: Orbis, 1999.

Younes, M. *L' experience mysticism et son impact sur le dialogue islamo-chretien*. Lyon PROFAC-CECR, 2009.

Young, Robin Darling. *In Procession Before the World: Martyrdom as Public Liturgy in Early Christianity*. Milwaukee: Marquette University Press, 2001.

————. *"Père Marquette Lectures."* In *In Procession Before the World: Martyrdom as a Public Liturgy in Early Christianity*, by R. Darling Young. Milwaukee: Marquette University Press, 2001.

Zubiri, Xavier. *El problema teologal del hombre, in Teologia y mundo contemporanec: Homenaje a Karl Rahner en su 70 cumpleanos*, ed. A. Vargas-Machuca. Madrid: Universidad Pontificia Comillas y Ediciones Cristiandad, 1975.

————. *Inteligencia Sentiente*. Vol. 1, *Inteligencia y realidad*. Madrid: Alianza Editorial, 1980.

————. *Inteligencia Sentiente*. Vol. 2, *Inteligencia y logos*. Madrid: Alianza Editorial, 1982.

————. *Inteligencia Sentiente*. Vol. 3, *Inteligencia y razon*. Madrid: Alianza Editorial, 1983.

————. *Nature, History, God*. Washington, DC: Rowman & Littlefield, 1981.

Articles

Álvarez, Andrés Beltramo. "Enrique Angelelli, 40 anos depois. 'Falta à Igreja argentina verbalizar a ditadura.'" *Instituto Humanitas Unisinos*, August 12, 2017. http://www.ihu.unisinos.br/565606-falta-a-igreja-argentina-verbalizar-a-ditadura.

Andya, Y. "Martyrdom and Truth: From Ignatius of Antioch to the Monks of Tibhirine." *Communio* 29 (2002) 62–88.

Aquino Júnior, Francisco de. "Fé–Política: uma abordagem teológica" (Faith-Politics: A Theological Approach). Horizonte 7 (2009) 13–31. DOI: 10.5752/P.2175-5841.2009v7n15p13.

"Argélia." Wikipédia. https://pt.wikipedia.org/w/index.php?title=Arg%C3%A9lia&oldid=64376683.

Ashley, J. M. "Ignacio Ellacuría and the Spiritual Exercises of IGNATIUS LOYCLA." *Theological Studies* 61 (2000) 16–39.

"Assassinat des moines de Tibhirine." Wikipédia. http://fr.wikipedia.crg/w/index.php?title=Assassinat_des_moines_de_Tibhirine&oldid=196041960.

Aveline, J. M. "L'écho de Tibhirine Chemins de Dialogue." 27, 1 (2006) Marseille.

Baudoz, J. F. "Le temoignage des sept moines de Tibhirine a la lumiere des Actes des Apotres." *Transcersazlites* 118.4 (2011) 147–59.

"Benedict of Nursia." Wikipedia. https://en.wikipedia.org/wiki/Benedict_of_Nursia.

Beozzo, José Oscar. "A recepção do Vaticano II na Igreja do Brasil." September 11, 2017. http://www7.uc.cl/facteo/centromanuellarrain/download/beozzo.pdf.

"Bergoglio e o papel da Igreja na ditadura argentina." *Diário de Nolicias*, August 12, 2017. http://www.dn.pt/globo/interior/bergoglio-e-o-papel-da-igreja-na-ditadura-argentina-3109545.html.

Bertrand, Dominique. "A corps pour Esprit; Essai sur l'expérience communautaire selon les Constitutions de la Compagnie de Jésus." *Archives of Social Sciences des Religions* 39 (1975).

Bingemer, Maria Clara. "La fe otra mirada para leer la historia. Una lectura en clave testimonial." *Revista Latinoamericana de Teologia* 27.80 (2010) 175–92.

Boff, Leonardo. "A recepção do Concílio Vaticano II no Brasil e na América Latina." *Leonardo Boff*, November 21, 2017. https://leonardoboff.org/2012/11/21/a-recepcao-do-concilio-vaticano-ii-no-brasil-e-na-america-latina/.

Borrmans, M. "Les dimensions culturelles et spirituelles du dialogue islamo-chretien." *Islamochristiana* 22 (1996).

Bouhdiba, Abdelwahab. "L' avenir du dialogue islamo-chretien." *Islamochristiana* 15 (1989) 87–95.

Brodman J. W. "Rule and Identity: The Case of the Military Orders." *The Catholic Historical Review* 87.3 (July 2001) 383–400.

Burke, R. "The Crucified People as Light of the Nations: A Reflection on Ignacio Ellacuría." *Concilium* (2003) 123–30.

Campos, Roberto. "O neobobismo dos jesuítas." *Folha de S.Paulo*, April 6, 1957. https://www1.folha.uol.com.br/fsp/brasil/fc060402.htm.

Casaldaliga, P. "Monsenor Romero estava en lo cierto, Carta a las Iglesias." *Año* XX.16 (2000) 446–47.

Casas, Gustavo. "Los jesuítas y la universidad." 3ª parte, Los Jesuitas y la Universidad. https://www.calameo.com/read/001043309eab51d91fd59.

Chergé, Christian de. "Chretiens et musulmans, nos differences ont-elles le sens d' une communion?" *Se comprendre* N° 85/04 (April 19, 1985).

———. "Conférence de Dom Christian, prieure N.D. de l'Atlas." http://www.scourmont. be/chagen/1993/christianfr.htm.

———. "Conference, Prieure de N-D de l'Atlas." http://www.saciourmont.be/ chagen/1993/christianfr.htm.

———. "L'echelle mysticism du dialogue." *Islamochristiana* 23 (1997) 1–26.

Clement, A. N. "Le fils et le musulman." *Chemins de dialogue* 33 (2000) 187–204.

"Constitutions of the Trappist Order." http://www.abbaye-montdescats.fr/?page_id=4.

Compañía de Jesús. "Reunión de los provinciales Jesuitas de América Latina con el P. General, Pedro Arrupe (Carte de Río)." Río de Janeiro, Casa da Gávea, May 6–14, 1968. https://pedagogiaignaciana.com/biblioteca-digital/biblioteca-general?view =file&id=1012:reunion-de-los-provinciales-jesuitas-de-america-latina-con-el-p-general-pedro-arrupe-carta-de-rio&catid=8.

Costoya, M. M. "A Reconstruction of the Theologies of Liberation: The Lacanian Corrective to the Ellacurían Synthesis." *Journal of Culture and Religion Theology* 8.1 (Winter 2006) 10–35.

———. "A Return to the Foundations of the Critically Oriented Theologies of Liberation." *Journal of Religion and Society* 8 (2008) 1–19.

Dande, S., and Christian de Chergé. "Moine de Tibhirine et lecteur du Coran." *Vies Consacrees* 85 (2013) 244–57.

Dom Patrick. et al. "Conformite au Christ at Grace Cistercienne." Conferences RGM, mimeo, 1999.

Durand, E. "Faut-il repenser la qualification chretienne dy martyre? Criteres theologiques et opportunite pastorale." *Transversalites* 118 (2011) 161–75.

"Ejercicios espirituales." Espiritualidad Ignaciana. https://espiritualidadignaciana. org/?option=com_flexicontent&view=items&cid=3%3Ablog&id=74%3Anon-coerceri-maximo-contineri-tamen-a-minimo-divinum-est&Itemid=3.

Elizondo, Miguel. "A visão inaciana do seguimento de Cristo" (The Ignatian View on Following Christ). In Reunión Ejercicios in Reflexión teológico-espiritual de la Compañia de Jesus em Centroamérica, San Salvador, (Dia 27,1), 1–8, Archivos de la Compañia de Jesús, Provincia de Centro America, Survey SJ de Centro América), apud Robert Lassalle-Klein.

Ellacuría, Ignacio. "Carta a las Iglesias." (January–February 1994) n. 297–99.

———. "Commencement Address." Santa Clara University, June 1982. https://www.scu. edu/ic/programs/ignatian-worldview/ellacuria/.

———. "Document. Textes d' un theologien de la liberation." *Ignacio Ellacuría, Archives de .Sciences sociales des Religions* 71 (1990) 85–92.

———. "El problema 'Ecumenismo y promocion de la justicias.'" *Estudios Eclesiásticos* 55 (1980) 153–55.

———. "El pueblo crucificado. Ensayo de soteriologia historica." *Cruz y ressureeccion: presencia y anuncio de una iglesia nueva* 32 (1978) 49–82.

———. "El tercer mundo como lugar óptimo de la vivencia cristiana de los Ejercicios." In *Reunión-Ejercicios de la Viceprovincia Jesuítica de Centroamérica*, 127–38. San Salvador: Survey S. I. de Centroamérica, 1969.

———. "Funciones fundamentales de la universidad y su operativización." In *Escritos universitarios*, 105–167. San Salvador: UCA Editores, 1999.

————. "Is a Different Kind of University Possible?" In *Towards a Society That Serves Its People: The Intellectual Contribution of El Salvador's Murdered Jesuits*, edited by John Hassett and Hugh Lacey, 177–207. Washington, DC: Georgetown University Press, 1991.

————. "A Latin American Reading of the Spiritual Exercises of Saint Ignatius." *Spiritus: A Journal of Christian Spirituality* 10.2 (Fall 2010) 205–42.

"Epiclese." Wikipédia. https://pt.wikipedia.org/w/index.php?title=Epiclese&oldid=6337 3615.

"Escola Militar Especial de Saint-Cyr." Wikipedia. https://pt.wikipedia.org/w/index. php?title=Escola_Militar_Especial_de_Saint-Cyr&oldid=59572422.

"Escuela de las Americas." YouTube, APROPOL - Asociacion Profesional Policial Santa Fe, July 27, 2008. http://www.youtube.com/watch?v=9e3LIXkVwW8.

Falla, Ricardo, SJ. "Oración a Ignacio Ellacuría." Instituto Humanitas Unisinos. November 16, 1989. https://www.ihu.unisinos.br/178-martirologio-latino-americano/573656-16-de-novembro-de-1990.

Farias, Andre Brayner. "A anarquia imemorial do mundo—Levinas e a ética da substituição" (The Immemorial Anarchy of the World—Levinas and the Ethics of Substitution). *Veritas, Porto Alegre* 53.2 (April–June 2008).

Flesher, L. A. S. "The De-domestication of the Cross: The El Salvadoran Experience." *The Living Pulpit* (April–June 2007) 22–24.

Geffre, C. "La portee theologique du dialogue islamo-chretien." *Islamochristiana* 18 (1992) 1–23.

Georgeon, Th. "Donner sa vie pour la gloire de t' aimer." *Collectanea Cisterciensis* 68 (2006) 76–104.

Green, Julien. La lumière du monde *(journal 1978–1981)*. Seuil (1983) 99.

Hemon, Ph. "Vers un A-Dieu en-visage de vous. Tempoignage personnel d' un moine sur ses frères du monastere de Notre-Dame de l'Atlas en Algerie." *Collectanea Cisterciensis* 58 (1986) 224–42.

"Iglesia: Jesuitas lanzen una carta contra el neoliberalismo." *Inter Press Service,* November 26, 1996. https://ipsnoticias.net/1996/11/iglesia-jesuitas-lanzan-una-carta-contra-el-neoliberalismo/.

"Ignacio Martín-Baró (1942–1989)." Universidad Centroamericana José Simeón Cañas, n.d. https://uca.edu.sv/ignacio-martin-baro/.

"Instituto del Hemisferio Occidental para la Cooperación en Seguridad." Wikipédia. https://es.wikipedia.org/wiki/Instituto_del_Hemisferio_Occidental_para_la_Cooperaci%C3%B3n_en_Seguridad.

"Irmão Luc, Monge e médico em Tibhirine." *Pastoral da Cultura*, January 22, 2015. http://www.snpcultura.org/irmao_luc_monge_e_medico_de_tibhirine.html.

"Jon Sobrino." Wikipédia. https://pt.wikipedia.org/w/index.php?title=Jon_Sobrino&oldid =60831954.

"Jorge Houston, hoje afastado do exercicio episcopal na cidade de Temuco, Chile, relembra, nos 30 anos do golpe no Chile, com misto de dor e satisfação, que "a união nos fez fortes e fomos bastante intransigentes." Terra, 2017. http://noticias.terra.com. br/mundo/noticias/0,OI140622-EI1782,00-Quando+a+Igreja+Catolica+desafiou+Pinochet.html.

"Justiça restaurativa." Wikipédia. https://pt.wikipedia.org/w/index.php?title=Just%C3%A7a_restaurativa&oldid=61723157.

Kaelber, L. "Molnasticism: Christian Monasticism." *Encyclopedia of Religion*, Gale Virtual Reference.

Kolvenbach, Peter Hans. "El Salvador" visit of the Jesuit General, DIAL 1298, (April 21, 1988).

"La escuela de las Américas: EEUU entrena terroristas." YouTube, January 28, 2010. http://www.youtube.com/watch?v=KXs09BlAxDQ.

Lassalle-Klein, R. "Jesus of Galilee and the Crucified People: The Contextual Christology of Jon Sobrino and Ignacio Ellacuría." *Theological Studies* 70 (2009) 347–76.

Leclercq, J. "New Forms of Contemplation and of the Contemplative Life." *Theological Studies* 33 (1972) 307–19.

Lee, M. E. "Liberation Theology's Transcendent Moment: The Work of Xavier Zubiri and Ignacio Ellacuría as Noncontrastive Discourse." *Journal of Religion* (2003) 226–43.

Lewis Thomas A. "Actions as the Ties That Bind: Love, Praxis, and Community in the Thought of Gustavo Gutiérrez." *The Journal of Religious Ethics* 33.3 (September 2005) 539–67.

Macedo, Suzana. "Louvor a uma só voz: Christian de Chergé e o diálogo islamo-cristão" (Praise with One Voice: Christian de Chergé and the Islamic-Christian Dialogue). MA diss., Federal University of Juiz de Fora, 2012.

"Martires de la UCA." Wikipédia. https://es.wikipedia.org/wiki/M%C3%A1rtires_de_la_UCA.

Mejido Costoya, M. "A Reconstruction of the Theologies of Liberation: The Lacanian Corrective to the Ellacurían Synthesis." *Journal for Cultural and Religious Theory* 8.1 (Winter 2006) 10–35.

Mendieta, E. A. de. "Le système cénobitique basilien comparé au système cénobitique pachômien." *Revue de l'histoire des religions* 152.1 (1957) 31–80.

Merton, Thomas. "Internet Bibliography." https://www.qsl.net/kc5nzr/merton/.

———. "Thomas Merton's Life and Work." http://merton.org/chrono.aspx#Biblio.

Michel, R. "Les rencontres d' Aiguebelle." *Chemins de dialogue* 27 (2002) 101–19.

———. "Le theme de l' echelle sainte en Islam et en Christianisme. La posture de Christian de Chergé." *Chemins de dialogue* 24 (2000) 129–31.

Minassian, M-D. "Frere Christophe, priant parmi les priants." *Chemins de dialogue* 27 (2002) 67–80.

———. "L'acte d'ecriture chez frere Christophe. Mouvement d' incarnation." *Collectanea Cisterciensia* 68.2 (2006) 130–46.

Naylor, P. "Bishop Pierre Claverie and the Risks of Religious Reconciliation." *The Catholic Historical Review* 96.4 (October 2010) 720–42.

Newman, J. H. "The Idea of the University." Newman Reader, September 2001. https://www.newmanreader.org/works/idea/.

Newman, M. G. "The Cistercian Evolution: The Invention of a Religious Order in Twelfth-Century Europe (review)." *The Catholic Historical Review* 87.2 (April 2001) 315–16.

Ochagavia, John, SJ. "Instruidos y pobres." *Revista Mensaje* 55.554 (November 2006).

Olivera, B. "Moine, martyr et mysticism: Christian de Chergé." *Collectanea Cisterciensic* 68.2 (2006) 117–32.

———. "Voici ta mere; I' experience d' un martyr contemporain; Christophe Lebreton." *Collectanea Cisterciensia* 68.2 (2006) 117–32.

O'Malley, John. "How Humanistic Is the Jesuit Tradition?: From the 1599 Ratio Studiorum to Now." In *Jesuit Education 21: Conference Proceedings on the Future of Jesuit Higher Education*, edited by Martin R. Tripole, SJ, 189–201. Philadelphia: St. Joseph's

University Press, 2000. https://www.bc.edu/content/dam/files/offices/mission/pdf1/ju7.pdf.

"'O Papa quer, em uma mesma missa, canonizar dom Romero e beatificar Rutilio Grande,' afirma bispo salvadorenho." *Instituto Humanitas Unisinos*, March 20, 2017. https://www.ihu.unisinos.br/78-noticias/565919-dom-rosa-chavez-o-papa-quer-em-uma-mesma-missa-canonizar-dom-romero-e-beatificar-rutilio-grande/.

"Padre Rutílio Grande, Mártir da Libertação dos Oprimidos." *Lendo e relendo*, March 24, 2017. http://ideiaspoligraficas.blogspot.com/2017/03/padre-rutilio-grande-martir-da.html.

Patrick, abbe de Sept-Fons. Conformite au Christ et grace cistercienne, RGM 1999.

Peninei Halakha. "Sins for Which Yom Kippur Does Not Atone." Days of Awe, Yom Kippur. https://ph.yhb.org.il/en/15-06-07/.

Pereira, Sibélius Cefas. "A Contemplação Como Resposta em Thomas Merton." *IHU OnLine* 460.14 (December 16, 2014) 52–56.

Phan, P. "Ignacio Ellacuría, S.J. in Dialogue with Asian Theologians: What Can They Learn from Each Other?" *Horizons* 32.1 (2005) 53–71.

Queiruga, André Torres. "Para além da oração de petição." Instituto Humanitas Unisinos, September 29, 2013. https://www.ihu.unisinos.br/524066-para-alem-da-oracao-de-peticao-artigo-de-andres-torres-queiruga.

Quinson, H. C. "Optimisme naïf ou invincible Esperance? Christian de Chergé selon John Kiser." Colloque Tibhirine de l' ISTR de Marseille, samedi 5 mars 2005. *Chemins de Dialogue* 27 (2006) 121–42.

Renna. "The Bernard of Clairvaux: On the Life of the Mind, and: Bernard of Clairvaux: On the Spirituality of Relationship (review)." *The Catholic Historical Review* 91.1 (January 2005) 141–43.

Romero, Monseñor. "Una clave de lectura testimonial." *Revista Latinoamericana de Teología* 27 (2010) 175–94.

Salenson, Christian. "Le martyre selon Christian de Chergé: contribution a une theologie du martyre." La Croix, November 15, 2006.

———. "Monastic Life, Interreligious Dialogue and Openness to the Ultimate: A Reflection on the Tibhirine Monks' Experience." *The Way* 45.3 (2006) 23–37.

———. "Parcours spiritual et theologique des Ecrits de Christian de Chergé." *Dialogue intgerreligiux monastique*, document 3, En Calcat (2005).

———. "Vie monastique et dialogue interreligieux sous le signe de l' escathologie. A partir de l' experience des frères de Tibhirine." *Collectanea Cisterciensis* 68 (2006) 105–16.

Sobrino, Jon. "El Ellacuría olvidado. Lo que no se puede dilapidar." *Revista Latinoamericana de Teologia* 27.79 (January–April 2010) 69–96.

"Socialismo real." *Interia Encyklopedia*, February 21, 2022. https://encyklopedia.interia.pl/nauki-spoleczne-humanistyka/news-socjalizm-realny,nId,1993179.

Sols Lucia, J. "El pensamiento de Ignacio Ellacuría acerca de procesos historicos de reconciliacion politica. Analisis de siete conceptos. Conflicto, Pensamiento." *Revista trimestrial de investigacion filosofica* 67.251 (2011) 103–24.

Souza, Juliana Beatriz Almeida. "Las Casas, Alonso de Sandoval and the Defense of Black Slavery." *TOPOI* 7.12 (2006) 25–59.

St. Ignatius of Loyola. *The Spiritual Exercises of St. Ignatius of Loyola*. Translated by Father Elder Mullan, S.J. New York: P.J. Kenedy & Sons, 1914.

Sullivan, P. "Saints as the Living Gospel: Von Balthasar's Revealers of the Revealer. Rahner's mediators of the Mediator." *Heythrop Journal* LV (2014) 270–85.

Teissier, Henri. "Ser igreja numa sociedade islâmica." *Concilium* 239 (1992) 44–54.

Trabelsi, M. "Le premier homme d'Albert Camus ou le retour au 'style' algérien." *Lendemains* 34 (2009) 157–68.

Tracy, D. "Literary Theory and Return of the Forms of Naming and Thinking God in Theology." *Journal of Religion* (1994) 302–19.

"Utopía y profetismo." *Revista Latinoamericana de Teología* 17 (1989) 170ss.

Vagaggini, C. "Liturgy and Contemplation." *Worship* XXXIV (1960) 507–23.

Vaz, H. C. de Lima. "Igreja reflexo vs. Igreja fonte." *Cadernos Brasileiros* 46 (1968) 17–22.

Veilleux, Armand. "Padres do Deserto." April 9, 1996. http://www.padresdodeserto.net/sequest.htm.

———. "The Witness of the Tibhirine Martyrs." *Spiritus: A Journal of Christian Spirituality* 1 (Fall 2001) 205–16.

Vitoria, Javier. "Chomsky, Romero y los 'mártires jesuánicos.'" *Cristianisme i Justicia*, March 28, 2009. https://blog.cristianismeijusticia.net/2009/03/28/395

Wilkins, Dame A. "Monasticism and Martyrdom in Algeria." *Downside Review* 126 (2008) 193–218.

"Yom Kipur." Wikipédia. https://pt.wikipedia.org/w/index.php?title=Yom_Kipur&oldid=62057488.

Zerh, Howard. *Trocando as lentes: um novo foco sobre o crime e a justiça* (*Changing the Lens: A New Focus on Crime and Justice*). Palas Athena, 2008.

Index of Names

Achaerandio, Luis, 121
Alberico, Stephen, 13
Albo, Xavier, 88
Amedee, Father, 24, 26, 38
Andrade, Father, 83n34
Angelelli, Enrique, 96
Antoncich, Ricardo, 86n46
Araujo Salles, Eugenio de, 83n37
Aristotle, 10
Arns, Paulo Evaristo, 96
Arrupe, Pedro, 86–87, 88, 89, 90–91, 93,
    94, 122
Ashley, Matthew, 112
Augustine, Saint, 12

Barò, Ignacio Martin, 99, 99n82, 100
Beauvois, Xavier, 3, 68
Beirne, Charles J., 121
Benedict of Nursia, Saint, 8–9n7, 30
Bianchi, Enzo, 133
Boff, Clodovis, 82n33, 83, 83n37, 101n88
Boff, Leonardo, 1–2, 20, 86
Boff, Lina, 1
Bondy, Augusto Salazar, 101
Brackley, Dean, 123n154
Buelta, Benjamin Gonzalez, 83n36

Cahill, Lisa, 2
Camara, Helder, 83n35, 96
Campos, Roberto, 89n55
Camus, Albert, 22
Cañas, José Simeón, 100

Cardenal, Ernesto, 84n40
Cardenal, Rodolfo, 100, 121
Casaldaliga, Pedro, 96
Casarella, Peter, 2
Castro, Fidel, 95
Cela, Jorge, 83n36
Chenu, Bruno, 67n146
Chergé, Christian de, 4, 13, 17, 17n34,
    22, 24, 26–29, 31–34, 33, 40–72,
    42n78, 128, 131, 133
Chergé, Gerard de (brother), 67–68
Chergé, Guy de (father), 40–47
Chergé, Monique de (mother), 68
Chomsky, Noam, 98n79
Clarke, Maura, 97, 103, 118
Claudel, Paul, 45
Codina, Victor, 86n46
Contreras, Manuel, 95n72

dall'Oglio, Paolo, 136
Day, Dorothy, 58
Derrida, Jacques, 69n148
Dochier, Luc, 24, 32, 32n33, 32nn33–34
Donahue, A., 8n5
Donovan, Jean, 98, 103, 118
Dulles, Avery, 19n35
Duval, Cardinal, 45

Eglash, Albert, 57n114
Elizondo, Miguel, 87, 111
Ellacuria, Ignacío, 1, 19, 80, 89, 91, 94,
    98–99, 100–126, 104n91, 128, 133

Estrada, Miguel Francisco, 121
Euripides, 11

Falla, Ricardo, 124
Farias, Andre Brayner, 62–63n130
Festugière, A. J., 10
Filochowski, Julian, 3
Fleury, Michel (Brother), 24, 37
Ford, Ita, 97, 103, 118
Foucauld, Charles de, 27n17, 34, 46
Fragoso, Antonio, 96
Francis, Pope, 52n112, 93n66, 104n91, 136
Francis of Assisi, Saint, 9
Francis Xavier, Saint, 114n130

Galaway, Burt, 57n114
Galtieri, Leopoldo Fortunato, 95n72
Gandhi, Mohandas K., 34
Grande, Rutilio, 97, 118, 119, 120
Green, Julien, 33
Gregory of Nyssa, 60
Gutiérrez, Gustavo, 1, 18–20, 82, 82n31, 86, 98, 101n88

Halakha, Peninei, 53n113
Harding, Alberico, 13
Hernandez-Pico, Juan, 111
Hillesum, Etty, 67, 72
Homer, 11
Hudson, Joe, 57n114

Ignatius of Antioch, 132
Ignatius of Loyola, 11, 15–16, 73–74, 74nn3–4, 87, 90, 110–15, 113n125, 115n131
Isabella, Queen of Castile, 95

Jerez, Cesar, 100
John Paul II, Pope, 24, 79–80, 83–85, 84n40, 89, 131n3
John XXIII, Pope, 102
Julius III, Pope, 77n15

Kazel, Dorothy, 97, 103, 118
King, Martin Luther, 58
Kiser, John, 24

Kolvenbach, Peter-Hans, 15n28, 88, 118, 122, 123
Ksentini, Rachid, 24

Larrain, Manuel, 96
Las Casas, Bartolome de, 93n68
Lassalle-Klein, Robert, 98n80, 111, 119
Lebret, Father, 82n32
Lebreton, Christophe, 4, 24, 31–32, 35–37, 39–40, 62, 128, 132
Lee, Michael, 106
Lemarchand, Bruno, 24
Lemus, Nelson Rutilio, 97
Levinas, Emmanuel, 47–48, 62–63n130, 62–66, 63n135, 69n148
Lewis, Thomas A., 17–18n35
Libanio, João Batista, 86n46, 88
Lima Vaz, Henrique de, 82
Lois, J., 83n34
Lopez, Amando, 100, 121
Lorscheiter, Ivo, 96
Loyola, Inigo (Ignatius) de, 13
Luc, Frère, 131
Lucas, Brother, 4, 5, 17, 31, 36–37, 36n52, 45–46

Mahiedine, Baya, 24
Maier, Martin, 123n154
Marx, Karl, 117
Mason, Mary Elizabeth, 10–11
Massignon, Louis, 34
McDermott, Robert, 7n7
Melià, Bartolomè, 86n46, 88
Merton, Thomas, 13, 27–28n18
Miville, Paul Favre, 24, 37
Mohamed al-Id (poet), 24
Mohammed (Chergé's friend), 41–42, 43
Molesme, Robert de, 13
Moltmann, Jürgen, 119
Montes, Segundo, 99–100, 121
Montesinos, Antonio de, 93n68
Montesinos, Vladimiro, 95n72
Moreno, Juan Ramon, 119–20
Muñoz, Ronaldo, 83n35

Newman, John Henry, 78–79
Nicholas, Gilles, 64–65n138

Nicolas, Adolfo, 15n28
Nobili, Roberto, 114
Noriega, Manuel Antonio, 95n72

Ochagavia, John, 73
Olivera, Bernardo, 24, 26, 36, 37, 40, 46,
    70–71
O'Malley, John, 74n6, 76
Origen, 11–12

Pascal, Blaise, 49n109, 62
Paul, Father, 37
Paul III, Pope, 77n14
Paul VI, Pope, 8n7, 83
Paul-Helene, Sister, 59
Pierre, Jean, 26, 38
Pindar, 11
Pinochet, Augusto, 95
Plato, 10

Queiruga, Andres Torres, 2, 26

Rahner, Karl, 98, 109, 116
Ramos, Celina Maristela, 120, 122n153
Ramos, Julia Elba, 120, 122n153
Ramos, Obdulio, 120
Ray, Marie Christine, 33
Ricci, Matteo, 114
Ringeard, Celestin, 24, 37
Robin, Marthe, 32, 32n33
Rocco, Editora, 4
Roger of Taizé, Brother, 33n40, 133

Romero, Oscar, 2, 5, 58, 80, 80n26,
    83n35, 92, 97, 97n76, 103, 111,
    116–17, 118, 131
Ross, Susan, 2
Rouart, Jean Marie, 39

Scatena, Silvia, 2
Scholastic, Saint, 8n7
Silva, Raúl, 96
Sivatte, Rafael De, 100n86
Sobrino, Jon, 1–3, 86n46, 88, 98, 99,
    108n107, 110–11, 115–16n133,
    115–17, 119, 121, 122n153
Socrates, 76, 128
Solorzano, Manuel, 97
Stephen, Saint, 13

Teresa of Lisieux, Saint, 43
Thomas, Saint, 12
Thurian, Max, 33–34
Tojeira, José Maria, 120
Torrijos, Omar, 95n72
Trigo, Pedro, 88

Veilleux, Armand, 25n8, 36n52
Vergès, Henri, 59
Videla, Jorge Rafael, 95
Vieira, Antonio, 94
Vitoria, Francisco de, 93n68

Yañez, Sol, 99n82

Zea, Leopoldo, 101
Zubiri, Xavier, 98, 105–9, 116